P9-DNV-134

A12900 241662

ILLINOIS CENTRAL COLLEGE
PS613.B4   STACKS
Bear crossings :

A12900 241662

PS
613
.B4   Bear crossings

WITHDRAWN

Illinois Central College
Learning Resources Center

BEAR CROSSINGS

BEAR
CROSSINGS

*An Anthology
of North American Poets*

edited by Anne Newman *and* Julie Suk

The New South Company
4480 Park Newport
Newport Beach, California 92660

66676
I.C.C. LIBRARY

Copyright © 1978 by The New South Company
LCC card number 78-55315
ISBN 0–917990–02–1

First Printing

Distributed by Persea Books, Inc.
225 Lafayette Street, New York, N.Y. 10012

Book Development and Design: Nancy Stone
Cover and Endsheet Art: Maryella Warren
Graphics: Pat Hager

also by The New South Company
*White Trash, An Anthology
of Contemporary Southern Poets*

PS
613
.B4

MARGARET ATWOOD "Dream 3: Night Bear Which Frightened Cattle" (first appeared in *The Journals of Susanna Moodie*) is from *Selected Poems*, Oxford University Press, and is reprinted by permission of the publisher and the author.

RUSSELL BANKS "The Poem Of The Year Of The Bear" first appeared in *Sumac* and is reprinted by permission of the editor and the author.

JANET BEELER "Feeding Time." Copyright © 1973 by *Antaeus* is reprinted by permission of the editor.

D. C. BERRY "Drinking With A Dead Bear" first appeared in *The Southern Review* and is reprinted by permission of the editor and the author. "Bear" first appeared in *The Grey Sky Review* and is reprinted by permission of the editor and the author.

EARLE BIRNEY "Bear On The Delhi Road" is from *Collected Poems of Earle Birney* and is reprinted by permission of the Canadian Publishers, McClelland & Stewart Ltd., Toronto.

JOHN CEELY "Bear" first appeared in *The Country Is Not Frightening* and is reprinted by permission of the author.

VICTOR CONTOSKI "The Bear's Blessing" first appeared in *Puerto del Sol* and is reprinted by permission of the author.

MICHAEL COOPER "A Short Story" and "A Poem For May Wilson" first appeared in *Fifth Assembling*. Copyright © 1974 by Assembling Press and are reprinted by permission of the author.

BRUCE CUTLER "Consider This." Copyright © 1974. *Friends Journal* is reprinted by permission of the editor and the author.

R. P. DICKEY "At The City Park Zoo" first appeared in *Rocky Mountain Creative Arts Journal*, Spring, 1976 and is reprinted by permission of the editor.

GENE FOWLER "Hunting Song" is reprinted by permission of the author.

SIV CEDERING FOX "The Cup Of The Bear" is from *Cup Of Cold Water*. Copyright © 1973 Siv Cedering Fox, New Rivers Press and is reprinted by permission of the publisher and the author.

ROBERT FROST "The Bear" is from *The Poetry of Robert Frost* edited by Edward Connery Lathem. Copyright 1928, Copyright © 1969 by Holt, Rinehart and Winston. Copyright © 1956 by Robert Frost. Reprinted by permission of Holt, Rinehart & Winston, Publisher.

VI GALE "Bear" (first appeared in *Poetry Now*) is from *Eight Poems*, Prescott Street Press, and is reprinted by permission of the editor and the author.

BRENDAN GALVIN "Bear and Misterwriter" and "Bear At The Academy Of The Living Arts" are from *No Time For Good Reasons*, University of Pittsburgh Press, 1974 and are reprinted by permission of the author.

PAULA GOFF "The White Bear" is reprinted courtesy of the *Chicago Tribune* and by permission of the author.

WILLIAM HEYEN "The Bear" is from *Depth of Field*, Louisiana State University Press, 1970. Copyright © by William Heyen and is reprinted by permission of the author.

JOHN HOLLANDER "The Great Bear" is from *A Crackling of Thorns*, Yale University Press, 1958 and is reprinted by permission of the publisher and the author.

DAVID KHERDIAN "13:IV:72" (first appeared in *Schist*) is from *The Nonny Poems*, The Macmillan Publishing Co., Inc., 1974. Copyright ©

by David Kherdian and is reprinted by permission of the publisher and the author.

GALWAY KINNELL   "The Bear" is from *Body Rags*, Houghton Mifflin Company, 1967. Copyright © by Galway Kinnell and is reprinted by permission of the publisher and the author. "Lastness" (#2 15 lines) is from *The Book of Nightmares*, Houghton Mifflin Company, 1971. Copyright © by Galway Kinnell and is reprinted by permission of the publisher and the author.

JOHN KNOEPFLE   "Tunnel Blaster On Bear And Brotherhood" is from *Affair of Culture and Other Poems*, Juniper Book #3, Juniper Press and is reprinted by permission of the publisher and the author.

GREG KUZMA   "The Dancing Bear" first appeared in *The Southern Review* and is reprinted by permission of the editor and the author. "In Love With The Bears" (first appeared in *The New Yorker*) is from *Songs For Someone Going Away* and is reprinted by permission; © 1969 The New Yorker Magazine, Inc. and by permission of the author.

DOUGLAS LAWDER   "Albino Bear" is from *3 Northwest Poets*, Quixote Press, 1970 and is reprinted by permission of the author.

DENISE LEVERTOV   "An Embroidery, I" is from *Relearning The Alphabet*. Copyright © 1967 by Denise Levertov Goodman and is reprinted by permission of New Directions Publishing Corporation.

ABRAHAM LINCOLN   "The Bear Hunt" (Canto Three 4 lines) is from *The Collected Poetry of Abraham Lincoln*, Lincoln & Herndon Building and Press, 1971.

AMY LOWELL   "The Travelling Bear" is from *The Complete Poetical Works of Amy Lowell*. Copyright © 1955 by Houghton Mifflin Company and is reprinted by permission of the publisher.

SUSAN BARTELS LUDVIGSON   "Trying To Change The Subject" first appeared in *The Nation* and is reprinted by permission of the author.

GERARD MALANGA   "we go out into the night" first appeared in *Truck* #12/*Vermont Anthology*. Copyright © 1974 by Gerard Malanga and is re printed by permission of the author.

MARK McCLOSKEY   "The Bear" first appeared in *The Contemporary Quarterly* and is reprinted by permission of the author.

JUDITH McCOMBS   "The Man" first appeared in *Poetry Northwest* and is reprinted by permission of the editor and the author.

JAMES F. MERSMANN   "Despair" first appeared in *Aura* and is reprinted by permission of the author.

W. S. MERWIN   "East Of The Sun And West Of The Moon" (1 line) is from *The Dancing Bears*. Copyright © 1954 by Yale University Press and is reprinted by permission of Harold Ober Associates, Inc.

N. SCOTT MOMADAY   "Blue" from "The Colors Of The Night" is from *The Gourd Dancer*. Copyright © 1976 by N. Scott Momaday and is reprinted by permission of Harper & Row Publishers, Inc.

MARIANNE MOORE   "The Bear And The Garden-Lover" in "Book Eight" from *Fables Of La Fontaine*. Copyright © 1954 by Marianne Moore and is reprinted by permission of The Viking Press.

Navajo Texts. Anthropological Papers of the American Museum of Natural History, 1933. "Song Of The Black Bear (Navajo)" (appeared in *American Indian Prose and Poetry*), is reprinted by permission of The American Museum of Natural History.

RICHARD O'CONNELL "Etude" first appeared in *The Paris Review*, No. 14, August 1956 and is reprinted by permission of the editor and the author.

JOEL OPPENHEIMER "For John And Lucy" is from *On Occasion*. Copyright © 1973 by Joel Oppenheimer and is reprinted by permission of the publisher, The Bobbs-Merrill Company, Inc.

KENNETH PATCHEN "The Orange Bears" is from *Collected Poems*. Copyright © 1949 by New Directions Publishing Corporation and is reprinted by permission of the publisher.

ROGER PFINGSTON "Two Stories About Cameras" first appeared in *Nitty-Gritty* and is reprinted by permission of the editor and the author.

W. M. RANSOM "On The Morning Of The Third Night Above Nisqually" is reprinted by permission of Copper Canyon Press.

KENNETH REXROTH "Bear" from "A Bestiary" is from *Collected Shorter Poems*. Copyright © 1963 by Kenneth Rexroth and is reprinted by permission of New Directions Publishing Corporation.

ADRIENNE RICH "Bears" is from *The Diamond Cutters*, Harper & Row Publishers, Inc., 1955. Copyright © by Adrienne Rich and is reprinted by permission of the author.

THEODORE ROETHKE "The Lady And The Bear," copyright © 1951 by Theodore Roethke is from *The Collected Poems of Theodore Roethke* and is reprinted by permission of Doubleday & Company, Inc.

JUDITH ROSE "The Bear" first appeared in *The Anthology From Women Writers At Hilltop*, 1977, and is reprinted by permission of the author.

DELMORE SCHWARTZ "The Heavy Bear Who Goes With Me" is from *Selected Poems: Summer Knowledge*. Copyright © 1938 by New Directions Publishing Corporation and is reprinted by permission of the publisher.

JUDITH JOHNSON SHERWIN "First Dance" from "Three Power Dances" (first appeared in *Painted Bride Quarterly*) is from *How The Dead Count*, Norton, 1978, and is reprinted by permission of the author.

DAVID R. SLAVITT "The Two Companions And A Bear" is from *Vital Signs*. Copyright © 1961, 1965, 1969, 1972, 1975 by David R. Slavitt and is reprinted by permission of Doubleday & Company, Inc.

GARY SYNDER "this poem is for bear" is from *Myths & Texts*. Copyright © 1960 by Gary Snyder and is reprinted by permission of New Directions Publishing Corporation.

WILLIAM STAFFORD "Sayings From The Northern Ice" and "Following." Copyright © 1960 by William Stafford are from *Stories That Could Be True: New And Collected*, 1977, and are reprinted by permission of Harper & Row Publishers, Inc, and the author.

LYNN STEELE "Ted Speaking" first appeared in *The Greensboro Review* and is reprinted by permission of the editor and the author.

JUDITH W. STEINBERGH "The bear ate the girl . . ." has appeared in *Consumption* and *Poetry: Cleveland*, and is reprinted by permission of the author.

JOHN STONE "An Example Of How A Daily Temporary Madness Can Help A Man Get The Job Done" is from *The Smell of Matches*. Copyright © 1972 by Rutgers University, the State University of New Jersey and is reprinted by permission of the Rutgers University Press and the author.

LEWIS TURCO "The Bears In The Land-Fill" first appeared in *Poetry Northwest* and is reprinted by permission of the editor and the author.

PETER VIERECK   "The Sleepdancers" is from *The First Morning*, Greenwood Press, 1972, and is reprinted by permission of the editor.

DAVID WAGONER   "Meeting A Bear" and "Song Of The Black Bear" are from *Collected Poems 1956–1976*. Copyright © 1976 by Indiana University Press and are reprinted by permission of the publisher and the author.

J. D. WHITNEY   "The Boy" is from *Tongues*. Copyright © 1976 by J. D. Whitney and is reprinted by permission of The Elizabeth Press and the author.

WILLIAM CARLOS WILLIAMS   "The Polar Bear" is from *Pictures From Brueghel And Other Poems*. Copyright © 1962 by William Carlos Williams and is reprinted by permission of New Directions Publishing Corporation.

ROBLEY WILSON, JR.   "The Marauder" (first appeared in *Poetry Northwest*) is from *Returning To The Body*, Juniper Press. Copyright © 1966, 1977 by Robley Wilson, Jr., and is reprinted by permission of the author.

YVOR WINTERS   "'Quod Tegit Omnia'" from *Collected Poems*. Copyright © 1960 by Yvor Winters is reprinted by permission of The Swallow Press, Inc., Chicago.

JAMES WRIGHT   "March" is from *The Branch Will Not Break*. Copyright © 1961 by James Wright and is reprinted by permission of Wesleyan University Press.

Prose selections:
ANNE BOSWORTH   "The Man Who Married A Bear," *Legends Of Wilderness Journey*. American National Enterprises, Inc., Utah.

COTTIE BURLAND   *North American Indian Mythology*. Tudor Publishing Company, New York, 1965. Reprinted by permission of Amiel Book Distributors Corporation, pp. 37, 119.

STEPHEN CRANE   *Sullivan County Tales & Sketches*, ed. R. W. Stallman. Iowa State University Press, Ames, Iowa, 1968. Reprinted by permission of Iowa State University Press.

WILLIAM FAULKNER   *The Bear*. Copyright © 1942 and renewed 1970 by Estelle Faulkner and Jill Faulkner Summers. *The Portable Faulkner*, Malcolm Cowley. Viking Press, New York, 1967. Reprinted by permission of Random House, Inc. An expanded version of this story appears in *Go Down, Moses* by William Faulkner, pp. 199, 200, 213, 318.

SIR JAMES GEORGE FRAZER   "Killing The Sacred Bear," *The Golden Bough*. The Macmillan Co., New York, 1951. Reprinted by permission of The Macmillan Publishing Co., Inc., pp. 586, 588, 591, 592.

ESTHER M. HARDING   *The 'I' And The 'Not-I'*. Princeton University Press, New Jersey, 1965, p. 39.

JAMES HILLMAN   *Jung's Typology*. Spring Publications, New York, 1971. Reprinted by permission of Spring Publications, Box 190, 8024 Zurich, Switzerland, p. 81.

ANIELA JAFFÉ   "Symbolism In The Visual Arts," *Man And His Symbols*, ed. Carl G. Jung. Copyright © 1964 by Carl G. Jung. Used by permission of Doubleday & Company, Inc., p. 234.

C. S. LEWIS   *Prince Caspian*. The Macmillan Publishing Co., Inc., New York, 1975. Reprinted by permission of The Macmillan Publishing Co., Inc., p. 181.

ANDREAS LOMMELL   *Prehistoric And Primitive Man*. Copyright ©

McGraw-Hill Book Co., 1966. Reprinted by permission of McGraw-Hill Book Co., p. 126.

A. A. MILNE *Winnie-the-Pooh*. Copyright © 1926 by E. P. Dutton & Co.; renewal 1954 by A. A. Milne. Reprinted by permission of E. P. Dutton, p. 14.

JAMES MOONEY From *Myths Of The Cherokee*, in *Mythology, The Voyage Of The Hero*, David Adams Leeming. Lippincott Co., New York, 1973, p. 284.

FLANNERY O'CONNOR *Wise Blood*. Copyright © 1949, 1952, 1962 by Flannery O'Connor. Reprinted by permission of Farrar, Straus & Giroux, Inc., p. 93.

THAD STEM, JR. *The Animal Fair*. Heritage Printers, Inc., Charlotte, N. C., 1960. Reprinted by permission of the author., p. 16.

JAMES STEPHENS "The Story of Tuan MacCairill," *Irish Fairy Tales*. Macmillan & Co. Ltd., London, 1920. Reprinted by permission of The Macmillan Publishing Co., Inc., pp. 19, 22.

JAMES TAYLOR *Seeing A Bear*. Poetry Bag Press, Pueblo, Colorado, 1971. Reprinted by permission of the author, p. 9.

J.R.R. TOLKIEN *The Hobbit*. Ballantine, New York, 1973. Reprinted by permission of Houghton Mifflin Co., pp. 118, 130.

MARIE-LOUISE von FRANZ "The Role Of The Inferior Function In Psychic Development," *Jung's Typology*. Spring Publications, New York, 1971. Reprinted by permission of Spring Publications, Box 190, 8024 Zurich, Switzerland and of the author, p. 72.

to Arnold, Bill, and Paul

A wild-bear chace, didst never see?
  Then hast thou lived in vain.
Thy richest bump of glorious glee,
  Lies desert in thy brain.

from *THE BEAR HUNT* by Abraham Lincoln

CONTENTS

FOREWORD

Early morning
  mist lifting.
Did you see the bear?
Where?
There (I think)
shadow crashing out of undergrowth when we least expect
  I'm dead!
  the girl screamed
  Dead!
It was chance.
It was the drum calling to the mask
the body dancing out of shadow
who knows where.
First the act
  the hunter throws his spear into a hump or hillock
later
  he is lucky in the hunt and brings home bear.
Now the shaman
  he who has suffered an illness
  and spends his life recovering
physician   artist   hunter of spirit
  he who describes the vision
" . . . and the vision is of great moment and beauty.
It has certainly to be believed in order to be seen."
Now darkness
  voices in a cave
  shadows flickering in the light of torches
the shaman wearing bear pelt and bear head mask
the shaman followed by a group of boys
  their bodies criss-crossed by strange markings
  sketched on with crayons of ochre and animal fat
the shaman stooping   crawling through narrow passageways
to the innermost sanctuary
  niches filled with bones and skulls of bears
  on the floor a clay model of a bear
  the skull of a cub between its front paws.

Now the ritual.
The shaman covers the bear with his pelt.
The shaman whirls a churinga over his head
and moves into the bear dance
  Right heel
  left heel . . .
Go home spirit.
Tell the other bears.

—Julie Suk

In *Understanding Poetry*, Cleanth Brooks and Robert Penn
Warren have chosen the word *bear* to illustrate the origin of
metaphor:

> Language did not develop in a mechanically "pure" form,
> without the contamination of emotion, but in a form that em-
> bodied and expressed the density of experience—the inter-
> penetration of stimulus and response, of object and perception,
> of idea and emotion, of action and feeling. The word for "bear"
> not only pointed in a disinterested fashion to a certain kind of
> creature, but also embodies "bearness"—the terror, awe, pow-
> er, majesty, and other qualities associated with that creature.
> Furthermore, language developed in a more specifically meta-
> phorical way by embodying the relation of thing to thing as
> expressions of human response and feeling. One thing might
> be like another in various ways. A man might be like a bear,
> or a bear like a man, not merely by, let us say, their com-
> mon ability to stand erect. A certain tribe might be "of
> the bear," and a member of the tribe would carry a certain
> "bearness" in him. Or the massive power of the stroke of the
> bear's paw might equate "bear" with "storm" or "storm"
> with "bear." The naming process might, in fact, embody such
> relations. When we find in the Anglo-Saxon poem *Beowulf* the
> sea being called the "swan's way" or the "whale's bath," we
> stand at a kind of crossroads: one road leads back to the nam-

ing process in the development of language, and the other leads forward toward metaphor as we know it in the formal poetry of highly developed literatures. . . . Looking back on the history of mankind we see that metaphor has been a natural—even essential—way of expression, and looking around us now, we see the same thing.

Metaphor related to the bear seems to be especially appealing to American poets of our time. Whereas bears have been killed off in many other parts of the world, they are still the most widespread of the big animals in our country; and to American poets they seem to have the combined appeal of the ancient and the immediate. Each poet included in this volume uses the bear in an individual manner; as a collection, the poems reveal a rich variety of attitudes and aspects of "bearness" in relation to man.

Our conceptions of most animals are generally limited to a few specific qualities: the fox is cunning, the dog is loyal, the deer is graceful and shy. We are amused by the antics of the monkey and awed by the ferocity of the tiger. But we cannot pin down the bear. This animal seems to have qualities almost as complex and contradictory as those of man himself. Certainly the bear has been a subject of interest to man throughout his history. In his detailed study, *Bear Ceremonialism in the Northern Hemisphere*, Alfred Hallowell concludes that "no other animal was found to attain such universal prominence as the bear, nor to have associated with it, over such a wide geographical area, such a large series of customs." This widespread interest in the bear is probably due to a combination of bear-man similarities and differences.

The bear resembles man in many ways: it is omnivorous, it assumes different postures, and it has a footprint much like a man's. Also, the bear ranks high on the animal intelligence scale. Edward Hoagland, in "Bears, Bears, Bears," attributes this superior sagacity to the cub's long interlude of intimacy with its mother. And Hoagland stresses other bear-human similarities of anatomy and personality:

Bears, which stopped being predatory some time ago, though they still have a predator's sharp wits and mouth, appeal to the side of us that is lumbering, churlish and individual. We are touched by their anatomy because it resembles ours, by their piggishness and sleepiness and unsociability with each other, by their very aversion to having anything to do with us except for eating our garbage.

The appeal of these qualities is strongly portrayed in some of the poems in this collection, and frequently the bear is used as a trope for the contrary or comical aspects of man.

But man also holds the bear in fear and awe. The tradition here is a long one. No doubt the bear's habit of disappearing under the earth for a number of months each year and emerging in the spring (the female frequently with new cubs) seemed mysterious and wonderful to primitive man. To him, the bear came to be a symbol of death and rebirth, of transcendence. He attributed special spiritual qualities to the bear, and often considered it to be an emissary from the supernatural world. These ideas, along with the great strength of the animal, may have initiated the myth of the bear-son. Discussing this widespread belief, Rhys Carpenter, in *Folk Tale, Fiction and Saga in the Homeric Epic,* convincingly portrays both Beowulf and Odysseus as bear-sons, thus relating the bear-son myth to epic heroes. Echoes and allusions from history, legend, and mythology are found in many of the poems included here.

The striking similarities and differences between humankind and bear must have promoted feelings of both identification and reverence which contributed to what Hallowell calls "one of the most constant and distinctive practices associated with bears, the custom of referring to the animal by some other term than the generic name for it." Some tribes, he has found, call the bear "elder brother" or "old man" or "grandfather," especially in conciliatory speeches of apology either before or after killing it. Other terms used are "big great food," "four-legged human," "chief's son," and "unmentionable one." All of them are considered honorific in character. That these attitudes of reverence and mystery are in a sense carried over to modern literature is perhaps most forcibly illustrated in Faulkner's great story *The Bear*, in which Old Ben is the center of the "yearly pageant-rite" of the hunt. Here the assertion of the timeless within time allows contemporary man to see himself spontaneously in the pattern of the past. Faulkner's references to the bear itself carry touches of an old sense of wonder. Richard Poirier has commented on Faulkner's bear in *A World Elsewhere: The Place of Style in American Literature*. He quotes from *The Bear* as follows: ". . . the old bear, solitary, indomitable, and alone; widowered, childless, and absolved of mortality—old Priam reft of his old wife and outlived all his sons." And he adds:

> Not merely the allusions . . . , but the style itself suspends us in time. It saturates us in a medium where objects are confused with the qualities of objects or with the values attached to those objects, so that "It" can refer to a cluster of impressions *about* the bear, while the bear itself can be named mostly by various abstractions, legends, and allusions.

In trying to group the poems, we found just how contrary an animal the bear is. As Russell Banks says, "You really can't count on the bastard / to be nice / all the time." We have placed poems which illustrate the concept of transcendence in the first group. Here each poet presents the idea of immortality or rebirth in his own special way; as, for example, through the ritualistic killing in Galway Kinnell's opening poem; or, as Gerard Malanga says, when the bears "enter our bodies and are born again."

In Section II, the bears tend to be representative of the unconscious side of man. Several of the bears are white, and they suggest an ambiguity similar to that in Melville's white whale or in the all-white pattern of Frost's poem "Design." Light and dark images interplay throughout many of the poems; and there is a strong sense of ambivalence in the combined feelings of fear and fullfillment; as when Judith Rose says, "I would embrace the bear/ with drowsy fulfillment/ he lumbers toward me"; or Mark McClosky questions, "What was it I saw lumbering/ toward the low moon as though it were a hive?" The quality of dream is frequently evoked in these poems.

The poems in Section III identify man with bear more overtly; the relations are more direct, conscious, and ironic. Thematically, the bear is used for some part of the nature of man; it may reveal the joyous integration of the spiritual and earthy sides of man, or their painful separation. In Delmore Schwartz's poem the heavy bear of the appetite pulls man down; but William Stafford sees the bear as representing the more creative side of man: "And Bear and I often went wild and frivolous." Bears in the poems of Section IV are quite "real" ones, but they also strongly suggest a prevailing sense of loss and alienation in modern man. Deprived of their natural identity and dignity, these are garbage-dump bears, circus bears, trained dancing bears, and others which show, as Lewis Turco says, "the craving of outcasts." And Peter Viereck sees in the bear "the deep sadness of a shaggy hope."

In Section V, the bears have strong survival value. Hoagland claims that "Bears have been *engineered* to survive . . . a bear's central solution to the riddle of how to endure is to den." Though all of the bears in the poems do not survive through such strategic retreat, they are tough, contradictory, unpredictable— valuable qualities in bear and man. In most of the poems, comical and fearsome aspects combine. Susan Bartels Ludvigson says, "When I tell him/ I've decided against him/ he laughs/ batting my wind chimes/ with his paw." Brendan Galvin's bear bites the hand that feeds. And P.B. Newman's bear "whales the tar out of anything he likes"; but he is "God of the high places and the groves." And Section VI celebrates this strong sense of vitality. These poems bring us back, in a sense, to the theme of transcendence in the first section, with, however, a special tone of rejoicing in the awareness. The bear, in many of these poems, is a metaphor for the renewal of life. In Robert Contoski's poem, the bear itself becomes a benediction, for "as the fur of my body has touched you/ you shall not be cold."

We do not intend to put any limitation upon a poem by placing it in a particular group. In each section there is a consistency of thematic approach and a rich variety of imaginative representation in subject, tone, and technique. The short prose quotations which introduce each group of poems suggest both of these aspects. The poems themselves are the best evidence of the continuing importance of the bear in the mind of man; and for those who may be interested in reading more about bears, a selected, but by no means comprehensive, bibliography is included at the end of the book.

—Anne Newman

BEAR CROSSINGS

All magic is but metaphor.
                        W. S. Merwin

I

Thus, for example, it is thought that if a Gilyak falls in combat with a bear, his soul transmigrates into the body of the beast.

"Killing The Sacred Bear," THE GOLDEN BOUGH
                                        —Sir James George Frazer

. . . the great, grim bear went bounding on heavy paws. I charged him at the head of my troop and rolled him over and over; but it is not easy to kill the bear, so deeply is his life packed under that stinking pelt.

"The Story Of Tuan MacCairill," IRISH FAIRY TALES
                                        —James Stephens

Old Ben too; they would give him his paw back even, certainly they would give him his paw back: then the long challenge and the long chase, no heart to be driven and outraged, no flesh to be mauled and bled. . . .

                    THE BEAR—William Faulkner

. . . and the shotguns and rifles which failed even to bleed it, in the yearly pageant-rite of the old bear's furious immortality.

                    THE BEAR—William Faulkner

My private opinion is that that bear was an unhuntable bear, *. . .*

        THE BIG BEAR OF ARKANSAS—Thomas Bangs Thorpe

The Bear

1
In late winter
I sometimes glimpse bits of steam
coming up from
some fault in the old snow
and bend close and see it is lung-colored
and put down my nose
and know
the chilly, enduring odor of bear.

2
I take a wolf's rib and whittle
it sharp at both ends
and coil it up
and freeze it in blubber and place it out
on the fairway of the bears.

And when it has vanished
I move out on the bear tracks,
roaming in circles
until I come to the first, tentative, dark
splash on the earth.

And I set out
running, following the splashes
of blood wandering over the world.
At the cut, gashed resting places
I stop and rest,
at the crawl-marks
where he lay out on his belly
to overpass some stretch of bauchy ice
I lie out
dragging myself forward with bear-knives in my fists.

3
On the third day I begin to starve,
at nightfall I bend down as I knew I would
at a turd sopped in blood,
and hesitate, and pick it up,
and thrust it in my mouth, and gnash it down,
and rise
and go on running.

4
On the seventh day,
living by now on bear blood alone,
I can see his upturned carcass far out ahead, a scraggled,
steamy hulk,
the heavy fur riffling in the wind.

I come up to him
and stare at the narrow-spaced, petty eyes,
the dismayed
face laid back on the shoulder, the nostrils
flared, catching
perhaps the first taint of me as he
died

I hack
a ravine in his thigh, and eat and drink,
and tear him down his whole length
and open him and climb in
and close him up after me, against the wind,
and sleep.

5
And dream
of lumbering flatfooted
over the tundra,
stabbed twice from within,
splattering a trail behind me,
splattering it out no matter which way I lurch,
no matter which parabola of bear-transcendence,
which dance of solitude I attempt,
which gravity-clutched leap,
which trudge, which groan.

6
Until one day I totter and fall—
fall on this
stomach that has tried so hard to keep up,
to digest the blood as it leaked in,
to break up
and digest the bone itself: and now the breeze
blows over me, blows off
the hideous belches of ill-digested bear blood
and rotted stomach
and the ordinary, wretched odor of bear,

blows across
my sore, lolled tongue a song
or screech, until I think I must rise up
and dance. And I lie still.

7
I awaken I think. Marshlights
reappear, geese
come trailing again up the flyway.
In her ravine under old snow the dam-bear
lies, licking
lumps of smeared fur
and drizzly eyes into shapes
with her tongue. And one
hairy-soled trudge stuck out before me,
the next groaned out,
the next,
the next,
the rest of my days I spend
wandering: wondering
what, anyway,
was that sticky infusion, that rank flavor of blood, that
    poetry, by which I lived?

we go out into the night

we go out into the night
there is a silence like rain in the glistening leaves
it is the time when the bears break out
from sensory instinct into something remembered
into something that darkens
their fur shines in the moonlight
they enter our bodies and are born again
as men crossing our headlights
clothed in bearskin and trying to speak

"Quod Tegit Omnia"

Earth darkens and is beaded
with a sweat of bushes and
the bear comes forth;
the mind, stored with
magnificence, proceeds into
the mystery of Time, now
certain of its choice of
passion but uncertain of the
passion's end.

      When
Plato temporizes on the nature
of the plumage of the soul the
wind hums in the feathers as
across a cord impeccable in
tautness but of no mind:

            Time,
the sine-pondere, most
imperturbable of elements,
assumes its own proportions
silently, of its own properties—
an excellence at which one
sighs.
      Adventurer in
living fact, the poet
mounts into the spring,
upon his tongue the taste of
air becoming body: is
embedded in this crystalline
precipitate of Time.

The Dancing Bear

They came down the road
in the early morning
dragging the bear by its nose.
They set up a small platform
in the square.
It was the sound of nails
being driven into boards that woke me.
I got up and had my breakfast,
and went out thinking
what will it be today?
Women with no hair,
unicorns, artifacts from
recent battlefields?

At noon a man came into the square
and stood up on the platform.
I recognized him as my father.
Soon he and the bear were wrestling.
Suddenly, before anyone knew
what was happening,
my father had pulled one
of the bear's teeth.

It was then the bear began dancing.
It danced around and around
the platform until it fell off.

Each year at this time
and later in the spring
we have these things happen to us.

The Silence of Bears

The silence of bears
is with me tonight
padding paws
over rainy rooftops
of the city

or in darkness
of the country
in drenched woods,
leaves lying on forest floor
forming footprints.

Water puddles
in their wet fur
but they are silent,
sleeping with noses
under imaginary tails.

I love the bears
with their silence.
They are like me when it rains,
imagining it is March
and about to wake up

with everything changed.

from *Two Stories About Cameras*

2
Smack on his back in the snow,
as if he might stretch his thick legs
to make an angel, the bear is dead,
stripped of stomach and fur.
The hunter, Yuji Shiramata,
takes a picture with his new Nikon.
It is his first bear and his last.
In two days another bear will tear
the focus out of Yuji's eyes
and leave him stumbling to his death
in Akita Prefecture. The bear
will sing of it deep in his throat
and stand on his hind legs
growling like an old man
having his picture taken.

Bear (Part Three)

Atop the rock hill, testing the air,
for a moment he will pause
black against the sunset,
painted poised on the world-wall,
movement compressed into form.
His stone claws reach the mountain-root,
his back-hump is one with the hilltop,
he is an outcropping born of the granite knob—

then swinging his head, rolling high shoulders,
he is gone beyond the ridge.
It is as if the mountain has moved.
Your eyes remain fixed on the summit—
you are afraid to stop watching.

Sitting Bear Mountain

Climbing in 3rd, then 2nd up N. C. 181
I see across the gap
the range I'm heading for:
Tablerock, Hawksbill
and Sitting Bear.

The mountains look like their names.
For years I have hiked out the trail
above Linville Gorge that ends
in an enormous configuration of rock
the eye converts to a hunched bear
who can be recognized for miles.

Always I scale his back
crushing heather and saxifrage,
clutching laurel, to rest on his lichened shoulder,
scared to look down. Always the voice of the river,
his own low rumble, I think,
tells me to go higher. And always,
terrified, I climb on up feeling
for a shakey footledge, a crumbling handhold—
his nostril? his eye?
I have never
once I'm on top of his head
been able to stand up,
ear-level with wind in eye-level clouds.
I know if ever I do,
I will become the hawk, the raven, the owl
that nests in the scrub of his fur.
If ever I rise
from my acrophobic crouch on his head
I will fly.

Always his river tells me,
you can do it, come.

Something in me knows
as I cling to the brain of the earth
inside his boulder head, then trembling
inch down to the path
that takes me back to my cabin
where real bears have twice
broken in to raid the flour bin
leaving comic, scary white pawprints on the rug—
something knows a real and present danger,
a real and present joy,
that someday I may stand and say *yes*.
I will go down the mountain his way,
launch out from the top of his head
into his tumbling voice—
never again gear down the S curves
telling him goodbye across the gap
as I always have
down N. C. 181.

this poem is for bear

"As for me I am a child of the god of the mountains."

A bear down under the cliff.
She is eating huckleberries.
They are ripe now
Soon it will snow, and she
Or maybe he, will crawl into a hole
And sleep. You can see
Huckleberries in bearshit if you
Look, this time of year
If I sneak up on the bear
It will grunt and run

The others had all gone down
From the blackberry brambles, but one girl
Spilled her basket, and was picking up her
Berries in the dark.
A tall man stood in the shadow, took her arm,
Led her to his home. He was a bear.
In a house under the mountain
She gave birth to slick dark children
With sharp teeth, and lived in the hollow
Mountain many years.
                    snare a bear: call him out:
honey-eater
forest apple
light-foot
Old man in the fur coat, Bear! come out!
Die of your own choice!
Grandfather black-food!
                    this girl married a bear
Who rules in the mountains, Bear!
                    you have eaten many berries
                    you have caught many fish
                    you have frightened many people

Twelve species north of Mexico
Sucking their paws in the long winter
Tearing the high-strung caches down
Whining, crying, jacking off
(Odysseus was a bear)

Bear-cubs gnawing the soft tits
Teeth gritted, eyes screwed tight
                    but she let them.
Till her brothers found the place
Chased her husband up the gorge
Cornered him in the rocks.
Song of the snared bear:
        "Give me my belt.
        "I am near death.
        "I came from the mountain caves
        "At the headwaters,
        "The small streams there
        "Are all dried up.

—I think I'll go hunt bears.
                    "hunt bears?
Why shit Snyder,
You couldn't hit a bear in the ass
        with a handful of rice!"

The Boy

       went walking
in woods.
His mother had sd
go
   find a good thing
& bring it to us.
He met a bear.
The bear sd
       boy
the sun is
heat in the sky
but
   the moon
is an old bald bear.
The boy
     saw it was a
good thing
took off his hair
& gave it to the bear.
The bear sd
       boy
open yr mouth.
The boy opened his mouth
& the bear jumped
           in.
Then he went home.

Resurrection Quatrain

When I die, I'll sleep
In your heart like a bear in a cave,
And come spring, I'll leap
Forth from shadow, the loving grave.

Poem Written in Winter

A dead black bear hangs on a weighing pulley.
Beside its silken hide, the nudity of carcass
is pink and public in the village sun.

Snow silences a deer yard for the hunter;
his bullet spins cold air with its kill.

Along the river, apples bait the traps
for muskrat, otter, mink,
whatever small breathes hungry under fur.

Through pond ice, trappers drive a sapling cross,
submerge a spring-device and popple lure.
Beneath the glaze where beaver swim,
it is one glide from life to drowning—
or waiting to be clubbed.

This poem is for the bear we have not seen
in woods behind our house. We feel its presence
sleeping under granite ledge. *Sleep on,*
we whisper from the porch.

Deer may outwit the hunter and not starve,
some pelted swimmers win their twigs or
apples staked above the traps.
When spring comes, we shall see who's left to browse
through safer seasons, go fat and easy
into water, hear laughter from the porch
when summer stars are countless,
the days till winter numbered.

March

A bear under the snow
Turns over to yawn.
It's been a long, hard rest.

Once, as she lay asleep, her cubs fell
Out of her hair,
And she did not know them.

It is hard to breathe
In a tight grave:

So she roars,
And the roof breaks.
Dark rivers and leaves
Pour down.

When the wind opens its doors
In its own good time,
The cubs follow that relaxed and beautiful
   woman
Outside to the unfamiliar cities
Of moss.

from *Lastness*

2
A black bear sits alone
in the twilight, nodding from side
to side, turning slowly around and around
on himself, scuffing the four-footed
circle into the earth. He sniffs the sweat
in the breeze, he understands
a creature, a death-creature
watches from the fringe of the trees,
finally he understands
I am no longer here, he himself
from the fringe of the trees watches
a black bear
get up, eat a few flowers, trudge away,
all his fur glistening
in the rain.

And what glistening! Sancho Fergus,
my boychild, had such great shoulders,
when he was born his head
came out, the rest of him stuck. And he opened
his eyes: his head out there all alone
in the room, he squinted with pained,
barely unglued eyes at the ninth-month's
blood splashing beneath him
on the floor. And almost
smiled, I thought, almost forgave it all in advance.

When he came wholly forth
I took him up in my hands and bent
over and smelled
the black, glistening fur
of his head, as empty space
must have bent
over the newborn planet
and smelled the grasslands and the ferns.

from *The Cup Of The Bear*

1
I have been driving
North
since noon.

A white line
pulls me.

I follow that white line

and The Bear.

2
A relative said, once,
to a child: look for
The Bear and find

The Star—you will always
know
your way home.

3
And The Big Dipper
stays there.

It scoops that liquid dark
into a dark cup.

It holds this vessel up
to the mouth of
The North.

Drink.   Drink.

I start somewhere
until directions
find me.

4
Where the river breaks into
white,
falling, you say:
I went to hunt The Bear.

But the orbit of the earth
threw me.

I stood alone beside
The Cross.
Altar and Triangle
mocked me.

I wanted to hold the animals
in my arms: The Lion, The Hare
—like this.

6
The Big Dipper was floating
in the vat of the heavens,
when I walked
to Helge's house.

Helge took a small dipper,
skimmed some cream off the vat:
Here, child.

Then he took a big dipper
and filled my bucket
with milk.

The constellation lost
its cup
and found
the larger shape
of The Bear.

That chased me. To run
and stop,
where I could see the light

26

from Helge's house,
by the milky way
of the snow-
covered river. I looked up.

The North touched the handle of
The Little Dipper
that poured
into the Big
Dipper.

7
Some night when The North
is heavy in me
I take the infant to the window
hold her high above my head
and say. This is your cup.

And when the buds of the twin-star
magnolia are covered
with ice,
I will take my son
by the hand
and walk, past the rowen-tree.

I will name the animals: The Bull.
The Bear. I will tell him
of the twin stars in the handle of
The Big Dipper
and how to find his way
home.

And he will stand there,
inheritor of space,
looking for his seven
sisters.

II

It ran in his knowledge before he ever saw it.

THE BEAR—William Faulkner

. . . participation mystique . . . *is a condition that modern individuals experience when they slip into the unconscious. It has been called the 'oceanic feeling,' and for many people it is a blissful experience, in which all responsibility is annulled. The primitive man's belief that the bear dance will inevitably bring the bear to the hunt depends on this unconscious identity, for the bear and the man are felt to be a continuum. And it must be admitted that sometimes the bear seems to feel it too, since reliable observers have stated that the bear* does *come when so called.*

THE 'I' AND THE 'NOT I'—M. Esther Harding

Then he saw the bear. It did not emerge, appear: it was just there, immobile, fixed in the green and windless noon's hot dappling, not as big as he had dreamed it but as big as he had expected, bigger, dimensionless against the dappled obscurity, looking at him.

THE BEAR—William Faulkner

The fourth door of your room is where angels can come in, but also devils!

"The Inferior Function," JUNG'S TYPOLOGY—Marie Louise-von Franz

Or in the night, imagining some fear,
How easy is a bush supposed a bear!

A MIDSUMMER-NIGHT'S DREAM—William Shakespeare

. . . *then [the bear] pushed on into the thick forest. It may sound odd to say that he glowed at that moment, that blackness. Ah, but he did, like a black sun, highlights and halos leaping from his deep fur. He was the light in the dark womb of the forest, disappearing into the cross-roads of Day and Night.*

SEEING A BEAR—James Taylor

On The Morning Of The Third Night
Above Nisqually

Images drip down my back like sweat.
From this hunger I can see time.
Dreams float in deep green whirls under that fog.
Four brown bears stepped through,
mist washing around them like steam
or old reluctant spirits.
We bowed in a ritual I did not know I knew.
A white woman stumbled slowly past
children bent her long pale back.
Her blue eyes opened like the sun
and two white scars sunk through my chest.
The bears shuffled close, shook their manes
and waved their heavy arms against her.
She dropped the children and they grew like gods.
Bear smell thickened, they backed around me like walls.
She touched the bears and they were stone.
She stacked them down there by the creek,
her children standing guard like pillars
and her breasts hanging golden in the sun.
She lumbers up the hill, low to the ground,
her hot skin wet under mud and matted fur.
Tonight she comes for me.

The Bear

I would embrace the bear
it is the coldness of his breath that troubles me

I would embrace the bear
his buddha belly

I would embrace the bear
his sleep face mask startles me

I would embrace the bear
I trust his roundness

I would embrace the bear
with drowsy fulfillment
he lumbers toward me

Plot

One writer needs something to cloak him
so he chooses the bear,
saying this creature recurred in a dream.
Another, getting on in years,
is quick to choose the tree.
It talks to him of death and he knows
we will see this, it being his trade.
A young girl picks snow.
It suits her purpose, charming us
into heat. Later, ice and storm will appear.
The moon is already taken.

I know how the story goes.
The bear tracks snow for his bounty,
marking sound. Snow glistens in the moon's claw.
The bear lies down on a trunk of ice,
taking the moon by force.

I lie down, not ice, not animal,
I lie down without cover in the branch of a tree.
And the moon lies down with no sound,
lodging itself in me.

An Embroidery

1
Rose Red's hair is brown as fur
and shines in firelight as she prepares
supper of honey and apples, curds and whey,
for the bear, and leaves it ready
on the hearth-stone.

Rose White's grey eyes
look into the dark forest.

Rose Red's cheeks are burning,
sign of her ardent, joyful
compassionate heart.
Rose White is pale,
turning away when she hears
the bear's paw on the latch.

When he enters, there is
frost on his fur,
he draws near to the fire
giving off sparks.

Rose White catches the scent of the forest,
of mushrooms, of rosin.

Together Rose Red and Rose White
sing to the bear;
it is a cradle song, a loom song,
a song about marriage, about
a pilgrimage to the mountains
long ago.
        Raised on an elbow,
the bear stretched on the hearth
nods and hums; soon he sighs
and puts down his head.

He sleeps; the Roses
bank the fire.
Sunk in the clouds of their feather bed
they prepare to dream.

Rose Red in a cave that smells of honey
dreams she is combing the fur of her cubs
with a golden comb.
Rose White is lying awake.

Rose White shall marry the bear's brother.
Shall he too
when the time is ripe,
step from the bear's hide?
Is that other, her bridegroom,
here in the room?

The Polar Bear

his coat resembles the snow
deep snow
the male snow
which attacks and kills

silently as it falls muffling
the world
to sleep that
the interrupted quiet return

to lie down with us
its arms
about our necks
murderously a little while

Blue from *The Colors of Night*

One night there appeared a child in the camp. No one
had ever seen it before. It was not bad-looking, and it
spoke a language that was pleasant to hear, though none
could understand it. The wonderful thing was that the
child was perfectly unafraid, as if it were at home
among its own people. The child got on well enough,
but the next morning it was gone, as suddenly as it had
appeared. Everyone was troubled. But then it came
to be understood that the child never was, and everyone
felt better. "After all," said an old man, "how can we
believe in the child? It gave us not one word of sense to
hold on to. What we saw, if indeed we saw anything
at all, must have been a dog from a neighboring camp,
or a bear that wandered down from the high country."

Dream 3: Night Bear Which Frightened Cattle

Horns crowding toward us
a stampede of bellowing, one
night the surface of my mind keeps
only as anecdote

We laughed, safe with lanterns
at the kitchen door

though beneath stories

where forgotten birds
tremble through memory, ripples across water
and a moon hovers in the lake
orange and prehistoric

I lean with my feet grown intangible
because I am not there
watching the bear I didn't see condense
itself among the trees, an outline
tenuous as an echo

but it is real, heavier
than real   I know
even by daylight here
in this visible kitchen

it absorbs all terror

it moves toward the lighted cabin
below us on the slope
where my family gathers

a mute vibration passing
between my ears

DENNIS MALONEY

The Great Bear

On an early winter night
two women went outside
to wash corn for soup.
When they saw Great Bear
silhouetted against an early moon
red eyes gleaming
in the lodge light.
Startled they dropped everything
and ran back inside.

Some men ran out
but saw no one
only large tracks
in the light snow.
Before dawn
the best hunters
set out to track
Great Bear.
They tracked day and night
till the trail led
to a great river
where the tracks disappeared
disappeared into the water . . .

Albino Bear

They say the white bear huge and thick
goes out at night when snow is deep
in the valley leaning its weight
on miles of fence until you hear
barbed wire creaking deep below
and then a crack   a shot as they let go
breaking   long lashing snakes
in the white underground.

They say his pale eyes darken to blue
at dusk as he watches elk plunge
through lakes of snow   winter mad to the bone
driving them to a fault
in the earth where steam breaks out
wazing trees with ice and the ground
is slabed thick with colored ice:
yellow sulphur and green copper salt.
From his mountain the white beast hears
the click of icicles clinging to their coats
the scrape of teeth and hooves carrying up
through sub-zero air as the herd makes the earth
give up its rare salt.

When he descends vapor gathers.
The moon comes in low to see how the bright land
will take her hot lapse off course:
the snow softening   shudders   land
collapses underfoot   steaming   the sound
of loose water running everywhere.

At dawn the bear gathers to him all his white children.
He scales the mountain with crust.
Cold moves in fast reaching hearts
of rocks to break them into cold dust.
Underfoot hard ribbons of ice run
descanting for miles to the bear
fallen into sleep and dreams rising
clear as ice.

WILLIAM STAFFORD

Sayings From The Northern Ice

It is people at the edge who say
things at the edge: winter is toward knowing.

   Sled runners before they meet have long talk apart.
   There is a pup in every litter the wolves will have.
   A knife that falls points at an enemy.
   Rocks in the wind know their place: down low.
   Over your shoulder is God; the dying deer sees him.

At the mouth of the long sack we fall in forever
storms brighten the spikes of the stars.

   Wind that buried bear skulls north of here
   and beats moth wings for help outside the door
   is bringing bear skull wisdom, but do not ask the skull
   too large a question till summer.
   Something too dark was held in that strong bone.

Better to end with a lucky saying:

   Sled runners cannot decide to join or to part.
   When they decide, it is a bad day.

41

Polar Bear

One eye open
the prone giant heaves
two thousand pounds
of matted sleep,
cream color fur,
old glaciers that leak
over panting rocks.
Storehouse of heat
suffering from his stores.

The White Bear

Not large, not fierce, and in distress,
A stranger to the South,
The white bear is running loose
In my past. I will go back
For a little while
Where everything is backyards and backalleys,
And almost dark,
Back to high fences and hanging gates,
Rusty wire on rotten posts,
Back to rows of yellow daffodils in black dirt.
I knew this place once.
The white bear is lost.
In his distress, he tramples the flowers,
Seeing nothing marvelous and strange
In yellow, nothing new in petals and stems,
Nothing needing protection.
He runs back and forth.
His eyes search wildly for something familiar,
Something white, like the North, and cold.
He knows nothing of warmth,
And is afraid.

I know nothing of bears.

I came here unexpectedly from my bed.
I had no time to be prepared. I wasn't dressed.
Perhaps it was my white nightgown,
Or the way I stood in the alley, also afraid.
Of the bear. Of the bear, I guess.
What can I do for this creature?
He's taken up with me,
Leaned against my side, given me his paw.
The paw is shaking. The fur is soft, soft.
I'll do what I can.
I'll do all I can for him
In my condition. I'll do everything
Humanly possible.

It's Bear Air

in the blue hills
pent, penny saw
the vision of great black
   and prayed
the paw subdued, moved
on through the night
   the river kept
its dark moon and
little charles dreamed
   he would attack
with vanilla ice cream
peacefully, he slept
   while penny watched
shadows move
across the chestnut grove
   to night's ridge,
the bear shuffled
down to where men called
   mad, against the dark
but penny had seen the eyes
inside her trailer would
   and giving names to things —
junebugs in poems, mountains
in april bloom, she could
   breathe now wild air,
warn the women of the hills
and face day's fright

The Bear

I heard the bear in the garbage. Would the door
hold if it saw the fire and wanted in?
My brush felt like cat's teeth in the dark;
I dragged the hem of my nightgown into bed.
What if it wasn't a bear, though? Wasn't sound
known to over-reach itself at night?
What was it I thought I saw then lumbering
toward the low moon as though it were a hive?
What woke me toward light that smelled so broken?

Feeding Time

Dusk again at the Old Forge dump.
Black heads honed with hunger
peer through the closing green,
then the bears emerge
furred in pitch shadows.

In this green light they seem to float
graceful as whales,
paddling at boxes of fish heads,
diving under crates of cabbage leaves,
their kitchen submerged in mist
and sinking deeper into the night stream.

My flashlight fixes two cubs in a fresh pit,
sucking on cider jugs
until their mother knocks them tumbling
to a treasure of beef bones
already sticking white as fingers
pointing from her teeth.

Grey muzzle, scarred hide,
fruit peel silver in his mouth,
only the oldest bear regards me.
He is the one I come to see,
and he drifts closer every night,
stiff-jointed,
his fur shined with slobber.
His flat black eyes
cleave to me as he eats.
After all these nights of watching
I have a place now in his hunger.

But what place has he in mine,
this great grey bear
stinking of fish and mud,
this enormous longing
feeding on my dreams each night?

Bears

Wonderful bears that walked my room all night,
Where have you gone, your sleek and fairy fur,
Your eyes' veiled and imperious light?

Brown bears as rich as mocha or as musk,
White opalescent bears whose fur stood out
Electric in the deepening dusk,

And great black bears that seemed more blue than black,
More violet than blue against the dark—
Where are you now? Upon what track

Mutter your muffled paws that used to tread
So softly, surely, up the creakless stair
While I lay listening in bed?

When did I lose you? Whose have you become?
Why do I wait and wait and never hear
Your thick nocturnal pacing in my room?
My bears, who keeps you now, in pride and fear?

III

. . . and many of them who dwell in the mountains pride themselves on being descended from a bear . . . and in the pride of their heart they will say, 'As for me, I am a child of the god of the mountains!'
"Killing The Sacred Bear," THE GOLDEN BOUGH
—Sir James George Frazer

. . . the way they squander about in pairs and single ones is edifying.
THE BIG BEAR OF ARKANSAS—Thomas Banks Thorpe

Well, you laughed to yourself, 'Silly old Bear!' but you didn't say it aloud because you were so fond of him . . .
WINNIE THE POOH—A. A. Milne

But wasn't he a beauty, though! I loved him like a brother.
THE BIG BEAR OF ARKANSAS—Thomas Banks Thorpe

The hunter lived in the cave with the bear all winter, until long hair like that of a bear began to grow all over his body and he began to act like a bear; but he still walked like a man.
MYTHS OF THE CHEROKEE—James Mooney

'He is a skin-changer. He changes his skin; sometimes he is a huge black bear, sometimes he is a great strong black-haired man . . .,'
THE HOBBIT—J.R.R. Tolkien

The lumbering bear swung his head of hesitations and thought again; . . .
"The Story Of Tuan MacCairill," IRISH FAIRY TALES
—James Stephens

Trapping Bear

1
If you live in the city, you will have
a good chance to catch a bear. Get a
bear trap first. Paint it white. Place it
behind some garbage cans.

Now, try to find some trace of bear.
If you find a bear, whisper something about
the nice garbage around the corner.

Only beginners catch a bear soon
after setting the trap.
Many experts never catch one. Some of them
even use traps that won't work—for the challenge.

2
You are close on the scent of some bear.

In a nearby room, a scientist is catching
the rarest bait in the world—
exotic centipedes and miniature eels.

To catch the fish to catch the bear.
At dawn he rows out to the middle of the lake.

You are going to your last stop of the night.
On the way you check your traps—rusted shut
just like you left them.
Bear tracks in the snow.

You turn and look into the grinning face
of a large brown bear. It places a massive paw
on your shoulder and speaks:
"Brother"

All day it has walked in your shadow. At night,
instead of a shadow, it is your bear.

Together, you enter your house.

51

Bear And Misterwriter

Bear came by, sat down.
Invited, of course.

Misterwriter not there yet.
Misterwriter not here yet, said Missiswriter.
She's kind of nice, Bear thought. *Bad legs tho'.*
Like chickens'.
Missiswriter went out the door.
Misterwriter, she yells. *Bear here!*

No answer. She yells again.

No answer.

Misterwriter comes in other door.
Sees me, Bear thinks, *but he's making believe.*

Misterwriter looks around, talking to self.
Bumps into table. Goes to spot marked X.

Missiswriter comes in. *There!* to Misterwriter.
He turns, discovers Bear on sofa.

Hellooo! Hand out.

* * *

Know all the constellations now, said Misterwriter,
Rigelgoose,
Betelgaff,
Glattstop.

Glattstop, Bear marveled, *that's hard.*

Not so, said Misterwriter.

No, of course, Bear said. *Try to be nice,*
                              Bear thought.

Tough, though. This time of year, Misterwriter said.

Really? said Bear.

Of course, said Misterwriter. *Too low.*
On the horizon.

Really? said Bear.

of course!

Change the subject, Bear thought. *What's that for?*
    Insulation?
Soundproofing?

Haaaa! Haaaa! laughed Misterwriter. *What could it be for?*

How do I know? Bear replied. Thinking: *Do I have a*
    bucket on my foot?
My wife made it, said Misterwriter.

*   *   *

If I like him, Bear asked himself, going home, *why did I*
    wave good-bye
with both hands?

The Bear And The Garden-Lover from *Book Eight*

A bear with fur that appeared to have been licked backward
Wandered a forest once where he alone had a lair.

This new Bellerophon, hid by thorns which pointed outward.
Had become deranged. Minds suffer disrepair
When every thought for years has been turned inward.
We prize witty byplay and reserve is still better,
But too much of either and health has soon suffered.
      No animal sought out the bear
      In coverts at all times sequestered,
      Until he had grown embittered
And, wearying of mere fatuity,
By now was submerged in gloom continually.
      He had a neighbor rather near,
      Whose own existence had seemed drear;
Who loved a parterre of which flowers were the core,
      And the care of fruit even more.
But horticulturalists need, besides work that is pleasant,
      Some shrewd choice spirit present.
When flowers speak, it is as poetry gives leave
      Here in this book; and bound to grieve,
Since hedged by silent greenery to tend,
The gardener thought one sunny day he'd seek a friend.
      Nursing some thought of the kind,
      The bear sought a similar end
      And the pair just missed collision
      Where their paths came in conjunction.
Numb with fear, how ever get away or stay there?
Better be a Gascon and disguise despair
In such a plight, so the man did not hang back or cower.
      Lures are beyond a mere bear's power
And this one said, "Visit my lair." The man said, "Yonder
      bower,
Most noble one, is mine; what could be friendlier
Than sit on tender grass, sharing such plain refreshment
As native products laced with milk? Since it's an embarrassment
To lack what lordly bears would have as daily fare,

Accept what is here." The bear appeared flattered.
Each found, as he went, a friend was what most mattered;
Before they'd neared the door, they were inseparable.
      As confidant, a beast seems dull.
      Best live alone if wit can't flow,
And the gardener found the bear's reserve a blow,
But conducive to work, without sounds to distract.
Having game to be dressed, the bear, as it puttered,
      Diligently chased or slaughtered
Pests that filled the air, and swarmed, to be exact,
Round his all too weary friend who lay down sleepy—
      Pests—well, flies, speaking unscientifically.
One time as the gardener had forgot himself in dream
And a single fly had his nose at its mercy,
The poor indignant bear who had fought it vainly
Growled, "I'll crush that trespasser; I have evolved a scheme."
Killing flies was his chore, so as good as his word,
The bear hurled a cobble and made sure it was hurled hard,
Crushing a friend's head to rid him of a pest.
With bad logic, fair aim disgraces us the more;
He'd murdered someone dear, to guarantee his friend rest.

Intimates should be feared who lack perspicacity;
Choose wisdom, even in an enemy.

Bear from *A Bestiary*

When the world is white with snow,
The bear sleeps in his darkness.
When the people are asleep,
The bear comes with glowing eyes
And steals their bacon and eggs.
He can follow the bees from
Point to point for their honey.
The bees sting but he never
Pays them any attention.
Tame bears in zoos beg for buns.
Two philosophies of life:
Honey is better for you
Than buns; but zoo tricks are cute
And make everybody laugh.

Following

There dwelt in a cave, and winding I thought lower,
a rubber bear that overcame his shadow;
and because he was not anything but good
he served all sorts of pretzel purposes.

When I met plausible men who called me noble,
I fed them to the bear, and—bulge! rear !—
the shadow never caught up with his girth,
as those talkers never caught up with their worth.

And Bear and I often went wild and frivolous,
following a way that we could create, or claim,
but we had to deal sometimes with the serious
who think they find the way when the way finds them.

In their deliberate living all is planned,
but they forget to squeak sometimes when the wheel
    comes round;
Bear and I and other such simple fellows
just count on the wheel, and the wheel remembers the
    sound.

The Bear

1

I was the first of us, leaving a downtown bar
one spring dusk, to see the bear.
I blamed it on beer.

It crossed the street to my side, deeper black
than the shut shops or near dark.
I tried to blink it back.

It passed an arm's length away. I stood straight
as a parking meter, and could scent
its long-slept lust.

I was the first of us to see the bear, the first to follow
its musky, rutting smell like a shadow
to its spring lair.

2

The beast's eyes glowed yellow on the stairs.
It rose to two legs and ripped its claws
across her shut door.

She led me quickly across her room, and bade
the enraged bear stand guard
beside her bed.

She pulled me down, and all the while
I felt its hot, fragrant muzzle,
until I heard her call

another to step inside the cage, the first to follow.
Later, the magic bear slept. As though
it could ever sleep another winter.

Tunnel Blaster On Bear And Brotherhood

you know him do you
why its true as Im standing here
he went off on a weekend
he thought hed hunt bear with his brother
but the bear ate his brother
and he shot the bear
he came back in here on the monday
with a bearmeat sandwich
wanted me to eat a half of it
see how a bearmeat sandwich tasted
I told him Im damned the day
I ate any mans brother
but he said there wasnt nothing to it
the bear didnt have time to digest his brother
ever hear of anything
ugly as that
and he throws the grizzlies marshmallows
Ive seen him sundays do it in the zoo

The Orange Bears

The orange bears with soft friendly eyes
Who played with me when I was ten,
Christ, before I left home they'd had
Their paws smashed in the rolls, their backs
Seared by hot slag, their soft trusting
Bellies kicked in, their tongues ripped
Out, and I went down through the woods
To the smelly crick with Whitman
In the Haldeman-Julius edition,
And I just sat there worrying my thumbnail
Into the cover—What did he know about
Orange bears with their coats all stunk up with soft coal
And the National Guard coming over
From Wheeling to stand in front of the millgates
With drawn bayonets jeering at the strikers?

I remember you could put daisies
On the windowsill at night and in
The morning they'd be so covered with soot
You couldn't tell what they were anymore.

A hell of a fat chance my orange bears had!

Ted Speaking

(for Fred Chappell)

KIDNAPED
$25 REWARD
for information leading to
Return of large Orange
Teddy Bear.
Equipped with inter-com.
Can hear and talk.
Call Lonnie Morris
926-0002
or Chief of Police Shelton

Listen, Lonnie, I saw that ad
                and I'm not coming home.
Count me out. I had it. You asshole.
You thought you had me, didn't you? Dragging me about
                in front of your friends,
Your face transformed. You punched my buttons,
                pulled my string,
Had me saying all those crappy things,
                "Kiss me, nothing makes me sick."
Oh, "Honey, are you a nun? (ain't had none and don't want
    none.")
                Damn, just who is dense?
My stuffings are leaking out. I'm done for but pleased.
I am my own bear.

BRUCE CUTLER

Consider This

Suppose that every soldier
sails, suppose that dollars
drain the deltas, suppose
—for just this once—that all
we meant had meaning: then

suppose that those commanders
come to judgment, the trigger
men, strategists,
and too the Congress and committees,
contractors, corporations,

then the planners and their plans,
the sycophants, the briefed,
the ones who wrote reports
and those whose herbicides
were spread and the body-counters—

and suppose that we swore to God
that only His own
sweet, effluent justice
move us at whatever
cost, whatever pain,

to an orderly withdrawal
to our own affairs, the streets,
the parks, employment, race
and money, and what we call
fulfillment of the self—

why then, consider this:
around the warmth of our
intent still stands the house
our history has built, whose walls
are law, doors decisions,

we enter now as if
fleeing from a lion
to find a certain peace,
but opening up the door
we suddenly confront

a great bear, pawing
the upholstery, ravening
in the kitchen after
bacon, honey. Consider
this, when you think of justice.

The Heavy Bear Who Goes With Me

"the withness of the body"
 —Whitehead

The heavy bear who goes with me,
A manifold honey to smear his face,
Clumsy and lumbering here and there,
The central ton of every place,
The hungry beating brutish one
In love with candy, anger, and sleep,
Crazy factotum, dishevelling all,
Climbs the building, kicks the football,
Boxes his brother in the hate-ridden city.
Breathing at my side, that heavy animal,
That heavy bear who sleeps with me,
Howls in his sleep for a world of sugar,
A sweetness intimate as the water's clasp,
Howls in his sleep because the tight-rope
Trembles and shows the darkness beneath.
—The strutting show-off is terrified,
Dressed in his dress-suit, bulging his pants,
Trembles to think that his quivering meat
Must finally wince to nothing at all.

That inescapable animal walks with me,
Has followed me since the black womb held,
Moves where I move, distorting my gesture,
A caricature, a swollen shadow,
A stupid clown of the spirit's motive,
Perplexes and affronts with his own darkness,

The secret life of belly and bone,
Opaque, too near, my private, yet unknown,
Stretches to embrace the very dear
With whom I would walk without him near,
Touches her grossly, although a word
Would bare my heart and make me clear,
Stumbles, flounders, and strives to be fed
Dragging me with him in his mouthing care,
Amid the hundred million of his kind,
The scrimmage of appetite everywhere.

The Bear

The bear puts both arms around the tree above her
And draws it down as if it were a lover
And its chokecherries lips to kiss good-bye,
Then lets it snap back upright in the sky.
Her next step rocks a boulder on the wall
(She's making her cross-country in the fall).
Her great weight creaks the barbed wire in its staples
As she flings over and off down through the maples,
Leaving on one wire tooth a lock of hair.
Such is the uncaged progress of the bear.
The world has room to make a bear feel free;
The universe seems cramped to you and me.
Man acts more like the poor bear in a cage,
That all day fights a nervous inward rage,
His mood rejecting all his mind suggests.
He paces back and forth and never rests
The toenail click and shuffle of his feet,
The telescope at one end of his beat,
And at the other end the microscope,
Two instruments of nearly equal hope,
And in conjunction giving quite a spread.
Or if he rests from scientific tread,
'Tis only to sit back and sway his head
Through ninety-odd degrees of arc, it seems,
Between two metaphysical extremes.
He sits back on his fundamental butt
With lifted snout and eyes (if any) shut
(He almost looks religious but he's not),
And back and forth he sways from cheek to cheek,
At one extreme agreeing with one Greek,
At the other agreeing with another Greek,
Which may be thought, but only so to speak.
A baggy figure, equally pathetic
When sedentary and when peripatetic.

An Example Of How A Daily Temporary Madness Can Help A Man Get The Job Done

My brother knows the man
who really is Smokey the Bear.
I have seen a picture of him
wearing his other head
and smiling his human teeth
into the camera.

Days
he feels, walks, sweats,
and talks to campers.

Nights
he lives in Memphis
under the name of Simpson,
sleeping off the woods
and the smell of fire.

Mornings
he puts on the fur suit,
and goes to work
only a little madder
than the day before.

It is the stares he draws
driving
that keep him going.
The hairy head
slips over his,
and the darkness closes
around him, deep
and comfortable
as a growl.

The Brown Bears Of Boston

With whiskers bent
from a vacation
of sleeping in southern log cabins,
the brown bears of Boston
stretch themselves,
jog into condition,
and find the road north.
They return to Boston
where they resume
their fierce existence
inside the bars
at the Franklin Park Zoo.

In Love With The Bears

To see them coming headstrong
battering the air
home to Goldilocks and three chairs
three bowls of porridge
three beds
taking the steps three at a time
barging into the rooms
this is what I grew up on
three bears with nothing to do
no terror of woods   each with
a small anger toward usurpers
that easy knowledge of something
taken and not returned
something broken and not fixed
something pressed
in which the hump still lay

Now years later I love them for what
they are
the common stutter of their fears
the worse stutter of their deeds
capable of being neighbors
capable of running for a short ways
essentially speechless
their fur hooked by thorns
wearing shabby coats
and passing in the street
sometimes glad to greet me
sometimes afraid to meet me with
        their eyes

IV

Creation rocked and the bear stumbled.

"Killing The Bear," SULLIVAN COUNTY TALES AND SKETCHES
—Stephen Crane

The bear went over the mountain once more, only recently. In lieu of whole ranges he saw more restaurants and hotels then there were spruce trees before the timber was cut, originally. . . . The bear saw a million sacred shrines straight from the heart of local history, or certainly physical illusions made historic by decades of fervent wistfulness. . . . The bear threw up. The bear threw up, in monumental proportions. And the news along the creek is he still can't take solid nourishment.

THE ANIMAL FAIR—Thad Stem, Jr.

. . . feelings are not only personal; they reflect historical and universal phenomena. They are common and collective. . . . not only something 'in' us, but also something we are 'in,'. . . . Loss is the main characteristic of feeling just now . . .

"The Feeling Function," JUNG'S TYPOLOGY—James Hillman

There . . . Keeuh lay. The bear had clawed away the great clumsy body she had worn in life. It lay about her like an old Bear's hide, and dead by the old stump was Keeuh, the lovliest young woman they had ever seen. . . . She would never wear the ugly bear form again and she would never hunt with Kut again.
Kut was like a man who had lost his soul!

"The Man Who Married A Bear,"
LEGENDS OF WILDERNESS JOURNEY—Anne Bosworth

. . . not even a mortal beast but an anachronism indomitable and invincible out of an old, dead time, a phantom, epitome and apotheosis of the old, wild life. . . .

THE BEAR—William Faulkner

The Sleepdancers

One crunch of fangs is all the thanks I'd get,
Were I to join the waltz behind their bars.
I tried to look away but shan't forget
This circus dance of sixteen mangy bears.

Their jowls, like good sports in a comic paper,
Grin their Indignity. Explore that word.
Your "injured and insulted," here they caper.
I wish I really thought they were absurd.

And do *you* think so, snout-chained soul of man,
You audience whose paws erupt that rumpus?
You middle-aged and grouchy, gypped of fun.
You growlers all, inelegantly pompous.

And tell me, do they sleepdance, just like you?
Nightly do they keep step, the whole sixteen,
When on the roof their plumpness teeters through
The canvas of the carnival-canteen?

Beneath the roof, their chainer is carousing.
If he but guessed what bear-hugs overhead
Flatten the moon they fly to when they're drowsing . . .
Suppose they crash? *Who shrives bears when they're dead?*

Shall cats and curs, that cringed to watch them lope,
Now dice to divvy and lug home their fat?
If I'm around, I'll put a stop to that.
I'll honor gaucheness anywhere I find it

And the deep sadness of a shaggy hope.

The Bears In The Land-Fill

These are their shambles: night falling
over the cascades of cans, broken jugs,
retired tires gone bald, inner springs
   come out into the fall. We sit still
   in the auto, waiting, our lights out,

   everyone's lights flooding the sky,
not a cloud to worship, the pregnant moon
giving birth to bone: starlight and moonlight
   over the land-fill. It is chilly
   waiting, the radio crooning to

   itself, muttering chanteys and
kyrielles under the dash. The watchman's
shanty blows in the wind, its shades flickering,
   watching for bears in darkness. And then,
   there they are in the naked headlamp-

   light catching them unawares where
they shamble in cottage cheese and horsehair
loveseats gone to seed: nothing to cushion
   the bare beam transfixing them where they
   hunt in the junk and offal. Only

   for a moment do they stand still,
limned against starlight. Then, when they turn from
the limelight back to limerind and orange
   peel, we get out of the car to stand
   among the bears standing amid our

   castoffs. We feel like castaways
in the dark of the moon, in the thick black
fur of the umber woods, a hunger in
   our hides—the craving of outcasts that
   the ravened land can no longer fill.

ROBLEY WILSON, JR.

The Marauder

When they shot the bear out of his tree,
North, on Monday, in Cedar County,
It occurred to us the bear knew, too,
Something was not enough—a stirring,
A yearning for sweetness buried deep
In the shrunk gut, portentous forage.
We knew and he knew: it was something
Not to perish of capture, sloven
And soft from caramel corn, smarting
With mange under the fur, with cinders
Lodged in the cracked pads. Something—at
                                    least
Not a cage—but not, truly, enough.
When they shot the bear out of his tree,
A single shot, and the limber trunk
Yawed with the target, sprang back, sang out
As green wood does in the springtime, stopped—
When the bear chose to drop, swam the air
Littered by yellow buds, pulled with him
The slim top twigs to the populous
Field—the tree bled; the earth at its roots
Shook and worms far under felt: waking.
For them, too, not enough, but something.

75

The Man

See, a small space in the woods,
green overgrown with green,
shadows trees brush entangled
At the edge of the clearing a man
a white man, middle-aged, aging
just his face stands out in the dimness
"dominion over every living thing"
a hunters' jacket, hunters' cap
He lifts the spear of his rifle barrel
aims
with cold, hard, arthritic hands
18 years on the line, finally made foreman
finally inspector, finally retired
The cold, square, aging jaws of my father
are barely flushed, a tingle of fear
or pleasure as he aims

diagonally across the clearing
into the black furry mass of the bear
She sits on her haunches, back to a stump,
an ancient, massive, dog-nosed brute
pawing the dogs
who yap & skitter away
(My mother's mother, huge in her dress,
sits in the creek, swatting the water & laughing)
She is warm, stupid; she smells of bear
an abundance of flesh, stumpy limbs
stone of a head & little pig eyes
teats where she rears, in the black close fur
She smells like my mother/my mother's mother
she does not understand
she won't get away

The man with the rifle aiming
confers with the other shadowy men
ranging the edge of the clearing
They have agreed
which one will have her
whose turn it is
one of them covers the kill

My mother does not understand
rears, paws, shakes her head & its wattles of fur
thinking she's won

Afterwards the body is hoisted
"a sack full of lard" on inaccurate scales
is hung, dressed, weighed on accurate scales
The skull (unshattered, unhurt) is found eligible
for Boone & Crockett official measuring
The head is stuffed & mounted
                                        safe on the walls
where every evening he enters, approaches
fires recoils fires into the small stupid eyes
"the thrill of a lifetime" my mother

Despair

Unseen she comes again
    sluffing among the tents
(even as the crowd cheers,
the calliope kicks colors
paisley in air)
the old she-bear, lumbers,
pauses at corners mowing the air,
lowers her head,
comes on

Circus-bear for the see-saw,
come home again to her delicate balance;
the added act; the held breath
of the trainer waits, watching
the shifting haunches, the uneasy level;
waits the sudden sheeny spasm,
the weight thrown from the clattering board
into the tearing crowd, the torn tents
collapsed in the desolate fairway.

AMY LOWELL

The Travelling Bear

Grass-blades push up between the cobblestones
And catch the sun on their flat sides
Shooting it back,
Gold and emerald,
Into the eyes of passers-by.

And over the cobblestones,
Square-footed and heavy,
Dances the trained bear.
The cobbles cut his feet,
And he has a ring in his nose
Which hurts him;
But still he dances,
For the keeper pricks him with a sharp stick,
Under his fur.

Now the crowd gapes and chuckles,
And boys and young women shuffle their feet in time to
the dancing bear.
They see him wobbling
Against a dust of emerald and gold,
And they are greatly delighted.
The legs of the bear shake with fatigue
And his back aches,
And the shining grass-blades dazzle and confuse him.
But still he dances,
Because of the little, pointed stick.

Muse

The roped bear's friendly enough there
in the littered yard. She does her neat tricks,
fetches the ball that she'll bounce with her nose,
lets the small, yapping dogs nip as they dance
round her. The flick of her claw is a silver
arc the broken dog inscribes in
the rectangular blue of afternoon.

I'm holding one end of the slack rope; the bear,
sun shining on its sequined ruff, shambles
this way, offering to let me teach her
waltzes. She wants music and the measured
step the ruff she wears was made to contain,
to dip and curtsy as birds do in air.

D. C. BERRY

Drinking With A Dead Bear

Sitting up all night with a dead bear
killed yesterday for dragging off
a sleeping bag with a boy in it,
I drink a shot of mash
and then drink one
for the bear, back and forth.

Going to the cabinet for another
bottle, I catch for my collar bone
swinging like a trapeze bar in slow motion
and recall the time Bear and I
danced in the circus
as cute as we could for sugar cubes,

toting our bag of tricks
back to the cage
when the spotlight was done with us,
giggling there in the dark
at how you had prissed off your left heel
and bobbled your head like a puppet.

Dropping the bag of tricks
and standing on your head,
springing back to your legs
in a half flip, paw on your hip,
reaching out for a cube with the other,
did you do it for the Ranger,

but get a sting in your chest
the way Cicero Luccachelli did
for the first time he missed the flying bar?

The Bear On The Delhi Road

Unreal, tall as a myth,
by the road the Himalayan bear
is beating the brilliant air
with his crooked arms.
About him two men, bare,
spindly as locusts, leap.
One pulls on a ring
in the great soft nose; his mate
flicks, flicks with a stick
up at the rolling eyes.

They have not led him here,
down from the fabulous hills
to this bald alien plain
and the clamorous world, to kill
but simply to teach him to dance.

They are peaceful both, these spare
men of Kashmir, and the bear
alive is their living, too.
If, far on the Delhi way,
around him galvanic they dance,
it is merely to wear, wear
from his shaggy body the tranced
wish forever to stay
only an ambling bear
four-footed in berries.

It is no more joyous for them
in this hot dust to prance
out of reach of the praying claws
sharpened to paw for ants
in the shadows of deodars.

It is not easy to free
myth from reality
or rear this fellow up
to lurch, lurch with them
in the tranced dancing of men.

At The City Park Zoo

Yes, I wish all these animals
were out, could be let loose—
but not just now, my car waiting
too far away at about 150 yards
and me leaning over looking
at the most splendid specimen
of an American Black bear
God ever created: cinnamon coated,
dumb, badeyed, and bowlegged,
he could still outrun this kid.

I've got the only part of him
I want, except I'd rather run up on
his enormous nobility in the wilderness,
be downwind and him not able
to spot me as I stood afraid and gloried
in his hefty super-teddybear brutehood.
Instead, I play Adam epigone,
call him Bruno (I'm not too bright),
and toss him a pound of cheap weiners.

I was out here one day
when the two timber wolves got up
on a high croon, kindling the dingoes
into similar yowls and curdling
my pink corpuscles into instant paralysis.
As soon as I could think, I thought
of Jack London—I swear I did!—
and myself alone in an old rickety cabin.
Later I asked the concession clerk
how often the wolves went into that act:
several times a week.

How badly
do I really want them out? Come on.
What articles have I written?
Who've I gone to see? What have I done?
I eat a chili-dog and think about it.

If they did let those wolves out
it'd take more than two of them
to tangle ol' Bruno off his feet.
But wouldn't it be something else
to come up on them in the woods somewhere
getting it on!
               They ought to let
them out, so they could take off
running, to their own places I know I
could never properly find, with my car.

BARBARA WINDER

The Polar Bear At Crandon Park Zoo, Miami

Panting, immobile, his head lies flat
in fly-buzzing shade, his brown eyes
shut against the glare. Before him,
pelicans and flamingoes strut brown and pink,
peck shells. Small children suck fingers,
watch him roll. His nose glistens.
His stink, his feces that were meant
to sink in snow, draws generations
of flies. One boy holds his nose.
The bear rises, swings his hulk
around to see the growing crowd,
cool in dacron. Concrete burns his pads.
His small eyes burn like brown suns.
From the ocean a quarter-mile away
he smells the cool of salt, the thread
that holds him through the long lizard days.

The Great Bear

Even on clear nights, lead the most supple children
Out onto hilltops, and by no means will
They make it out. Neither the gruff round image
From a remembered page nor the uncertain
Finger, tracing that image out, can manage
To mark the lines of what ought to be there,
Passing through certain bounding stars until
The whole massive expanse of bear appear
Swinging, across the ecliptic, and although
The littlest ones say nothing, others respond,
Making us thankful in varying degrees
For what we would have shown them: "There it is!"
"I see it now!" Even "Very like a bear!"
Would make us grateful. Because there is no bear,

We blame our memory of the picture. Trudging
Up the dark, starlit path, stooping to clutch
An anxious hand, perhaps the outline faded
Then; perhaps, could we have retained the thing
In mind ourselves, with it we might have staged
Something convincing. We easily forget
The huge, clear, homely dipper that is such
An event to reckon with, an object set
Across the space the bear should occupy;
But, even so, the trouble lies in pointing
At any stars. For one's own finger aims
Always elsewhere; the man beside one seems
Never to get the point. "No! The bright star
Just above my fingertip." The star,

If any, that he sees beyond one's finger
Will never be the intended one. To bring
Another's eye to bear in such a fashion
On any single star seems to require
Something very like a constellation
That both habitually see at night;
Not in the stars themselves but in among
Their scatter, perhaps, some old familiar sight
Is always there to take a bearing from.
And if the smallest child of all should cry
Out on the wet black grass because he sees
Nothing but stars, though claiming that there is
Some bear not there that frightens him, we need
Only reflect that we ourselves have need

Of what is fearful (being really nothing),
With which to find our way about the path
That leads back down the hill again, and with
Which to enable the older children, standing
By us, to follow what we mean by "This
Star," "That one," "The other one beyond it."
But what of the tiny, scared ones?—Such a bear—
Who needs it? We can still make do with both
The dipper that we always knew was there
And the bright, simple shapes that suddenly
Emerge on certain nights. To understand
The signs that stars compose, we need depend
Only on stars that are entirely there
And the apparent space between them. There

Never need be lines between them, puzzling
Our sense of what is what. What a star does
Is never to surprise us as it covers
The center of its patch of darkness, sparkling
Always, a point in one of many figures.
One solitary star would be quite useless,
A frigid conjecture, true but trifling,

And any single sign is meaningless
If unnecessary. Crab, bull, and ram,
Or frosty irregular polygons of our own
Devising, or, finally, the Great Dark Bear
That we can never quite believe is there—
Having the others, any one of them
Can be dispensed with. The Bear, of all of them,
Is somehow most like any one, taken
At random, in that we always tend to say
That just because it might be there, because
Some Ancients really traced it out, a broken
And complicated line, webbing bright stars
And fainter ones together, because a bear
Habitually appeared, then even by day
It is for us a thing that should be there.
We should not want to train ourselves to see it.
The world is everything that happens to
Be true. The stars at night seem to suggest
The shapes of what might be. If it were best,
Even, to have it there (Such a great bear!
All hung with stars!), there still would be no bear.

V

'We have given you food and joy and health; now we kill you in order that you may in return send riches to us and to our children.' To this discourse the bear, more and more surly and agitated, listens without conviction; round and round the tree he paces and howls lamentably, . . .

"Killing The Sacred Bear," THE GOLDEN BOUGH
—Sir James George Frazer

If exasperated in close quarters, a bear may let drive savagely with both paws and snarl and bite with great fierceness. In this case, it is advisable to retire, if convenient.

"Sullivan County Bears,"
SULLIVAN COUNTY TALES AND SKETCHES—Stephen Crane

As Rhpisunt was walking up into the hills she stepped on a bear's excrement and her foot was smeared. This made her very angry: she said 'This bear was a dirty beast and heedless of where I, a lady, stepped, as if it were somebody important.' She kept grumbling about this all day; whenever she saw one of her friends she would shout out angry remarks about the bears.

NORTH AMERICAN INDIAN MYTHOLOGY—Cottie Burland

He pulled Haze toward the cages. Two black bears sat in the first one, facing each other like two matrons having tea, their faces polite and self-absorbed. 'They don't do nothing but sit there all day and stink,' Enoch said.

WISE BLOOD—Flannery O'Connor

'He's a good creature, but he'll shame us all. He'll go to sleep and he will suck his paws. In front of the enemy too'. . . . The Bear whipped its paw out of its mouth and pretended it hadn't heard.

PRINCE CASPIAN—C. S. Lewis

Bear At The Academy Of The Living Arts

Got there early.

Women the color of preserved baby shoes
kept trying to knock Bear down
with their big eyelashes.
Athens, says one. *Rome,* argues another.

They were blowing
up the president of the Academy.
Bicycle pump in his belly button.

More air to the bow tie, said the lady
with big glasses on.

He's very high-powered, she said to Bear.
What do you do?

Big eyes, she had.
Bear kept his hands at sides.
Organs collapsed inside.

Rub my ass on trees? Can't tell her that,
                             Bear thought.

Eat blueberries and sleep? Nix on that, too.

Bite the hand, Bear said. *Feeds me.*
Oops. Slipped out. Bear's hand over mouth too late.

What they call you? asked she,
                             smile all hung out.

Stud, Bear lied.
Stub, laughed she, *tha's cute.*

from *The Poem Of The Year Of The Bear*

You really can't count on the bastard
to be nice
all the time.
                    There are days,
        high, hollow days that keep drifting back like clouds
        in spring, when the bear rambles down hills
        and thinks of nothing
        but tearing into some glistening roan mare's side—
                keeps checking claws hopefully
                for drops of blood.
                                    There are days
        in spring when the smell of teen-aged cunt
            drifts up smokily through black spruce and broken rock
                to where the bear sits dreaming of orchestras,
                and when that grey wet musk has got up
                            behind tiny eyes, it eats at him
                as if ants had clotted together back there,
                driving him down
                                    first to the warming slopes
        then to the very source,
                                    which he reaches by nightfall—
            tongue red and stiffly drooling,
            eyes hardened to crystal now,
    and thickened claws sloppily rending taut canvas sides of tents,
                    bear moaning like a cut moon,
                sticking his waggling prick ahead of him as the girls
                    stuff their mouths and ears
                    with fingers yanked from hot boxes,
                    sit on their smells and scream
                    for hatchets
                    and large barking dogs.
                Sprays everything across the bare ground,
                and the bear sags, groans bitterly,
                knows that now

94

he's got to squat and talk about it
with these serious young ladies from Ohio
till dawn spreads on still lower slopes like a milky smear
and the boys return from fishing smelt with soft nets
silently, in the fading dark returning.
The girls'll tell 'em over breakfast
how they ought to pity the bear,
the bear, the drunk and rambling bear
as he drifts slowly back up the mountain
cruising behind the rising mists,
eyes puffied and sliding side to side,
claws drawn back to elbows,
and prick buried somewhere deep
between his thighs like a womb,
wrinkled and black.

Bear

often called   man's half
brother and beast-self
has taken of late
to doing   the unheard-of
in his woods
HE
gnaws live bark   girdles trunks
baffles the naturalist   upsets an eco-system
KILLS TREES

the bear ate the girl
she wasn't dead
ate her in large bites
bears have
large appetites
ate her like a child
eats a donut
ate her parts
away
she saw her arm
lying quite alone
a yard away
she heard the crunch
of bones, the munching up
of flesh
she said
he's got my arm
I'm dead

DAVID WAGONER

Meeting A Bear

If you haven't made noise enough to warn him, singing, shouting,
Or thumping sticks against trees as you walk in the woods,
Giving him time to vanish
(As he wants to) quietly sideways through the nearest thicket,
You may wind up standing face to face with a bear.
Your near future,
Even your distant future, may depend on how he feels
Looking at you, on what he makes of you
And your upright posture
Which, in his world, like a down-swayed head and humped
    shoulders,
Is a standing offer to fight for territory
And a mate to go with it.
Gaping and staring directly are as risky as running:
To try for dominance or moral authority
Is an empty gesture,
And taking to your heels is an invitation to a dance
Which, from your point of view, will be no circus.
He won't enjoy your smell
Or anything else about you, including your ancestors
Or the shape of your snout. If the feeling's mutual,
It's still out of balance:
He doesn't *care* what you think or calculate; your disapproval
Leaves him as cold as the opinions of salmon.
He may feel free
To act out all his own displeasures with a vengeance:
You would do well to try your meekest behavior,
Standing still
As long as you're not mauled or hugged, your eyes downcast.
But if you must make a stir, do everything sidelong,
Gently and naturally,
Vaguely oblique. Withdraw without turning and start saying
Softly, monotonously, whatever comes to mind
Without special pleading:

98

Nothing hurt or reproachful to appeal to his better feelings.
He has none, only a harder life than yours.
There's no use singing
National anthems or battle hymns or alma maters
Or any other charming or beastly music.
Use only the dullest,
Blandest, most colorless, undemonstrative speech you can think
    of,
Bears, for good reason, find it embarrassing
Or at least disarming
And will forget their claws and cover their eyeteeth as an answer.
Meanwhile, move off, yielding the forest floor
As carefully as your honor.

Bear

Bear
was in the back of my mind
as I walked up the logging road

when I meet
        a black bear
                like somebody's giant poodle romping down on me

wheels,
scared giddy,

barrels into thicket
        pounding the pine needles,   sticks popping
                bushes whipping him,

gallops like 70 poodles only faster
whistling
            sharp
                    out-breaths,
disappears.

I didn't move.

DAVID SLAVITT

Two Companions And The Bear

(IX—The Fables of Avianus)

The road dark, the country wild, the pair
already terrified, the hungry bear
was more than a mere projection of their mood,
but shaggy with lumbering life and out for blood.
One of the travelers, lucky or quick, ascended
a tree, but the other, alone after what his friend did,
collapsed on the spot, played possum, became a ball
of helpless flesh desiring to be small.
The bear approached and with an inquiring nose
poked at his obstinate bulk, while his blood froze.
It hesitated. No bear wants to eat
carrion, after all. With one of its feet
it prodded the quondam tidbit, and then went off.
From up in the tree, a tactful, inquiring cough,
and: "You all right?"
                        The blood thawed and flowed,
and the supine fellow picked himself up from the road.
"A hell of a thing," said the one coming down from the tree.
"It was," said the other. "You know what the bear said to
me?"
"It *said*? It spoke? What did it say?"
                                        "To end
my association with you, you no-good, son-of-a-bitch,
    piss-ant bastard excuse for a friend."

The Lady And The Bear

A Lady came to a Bear by a Stream.
"O why are you fishing that way?
Tell me, dear Bear there by the Stream,
Why are you fishing that way?"

"I am what is known as a Biddly Bear,—
That's why I'm fishing this way.
We Biddly's are Pee-culiar Bears.
And so,—I'm fishing this way.

"And besides, it seems there's a Law:
A most, most exactious Law
Says a Bear
Doesn't dare
Doesn't dare
Doesn't DARE
Use a Hook or a Line,
Or an old piece of Twine,
Not even the end of his Claw, Claw, Claw,
Not even the end of his Claw.
Yes, a Bear has to fish with his Paw, Paw, Paw.
A Bear has to fish with his Paw."

"O it's Wonderful how with a flick of your Wrist,
You can fish out a fish, out a fish, out a fish,
If *I* were a fish I just couldn't resist
You, when you are fishing that way, that way,
When you are fishing that way."

And at that the Lady slipped from the Bank
And fell in the Stream still clutching a Plank,
But the Bear just sat there until she Sank
As he went on fishing his way, his way,
As he went on fishing his way.

Trying To Change The Subject

I have sworn to quit
inviting antelope
and elk
into my small back yard,
but the bear refuses
to stop wandering in.
His fur
always gets caught
in the gate
and his steps
on the porch
rattle the glasses
in my cupboard.
Each time he comes
the dog is nervous
for a week.
When he ate my blackberries
I said it didn't matter
but in fact
I had nothing to eat
all day. Yet
when I tell him
I've decided against him,
he laughs,
batting my wind chimes
with his paw.

A Short Story

very happy. It was a matter of totally differe
just couldn't relate as people any longer. Liv
cabin in the woods with grandma was diff
with the bears. I lacked a playmate. The abs
family life was also a strain. Alone with
the time, I had bad feelings. I came to th
abandoned, neglected, a sort of waif. I d
slight squint.

It had to be so, for the bears had all mov
and Grandma, who had meant to be swee
when tending to the needs of a small child li
nearly all of her energies. There was, in
real contact between us. It came out in th
her for intruding on me by bringing me b
and she, though probably meaning to be
me at a certain distance, as if still fearful
I was trying to lead.

Wringing her hands, she used to say, "If
were still living. It's so sad. So sad, so sad,
tell you it's just plain sad. . . ."

A Poem For May Wilson

I say the oms relating bring into teddy once
I love the huh people to people of teddy here
I do uh what relating a spell and a box
I do bro trouble people them and brooms group here
I say use trouble I had old dolls into my age once
I love had what and tossed old dolls of my age bears
I only had oms with them me my age once
I've use huh with a spell in a box bears
I've bro same and toss bring in brooms bears
I only uh same I had to people me a box

D. C. BERRY

Bear

(For John Mays)

700 pounds, no neck,
bullet eyes,
eats our April birthday cake,
follows his muck
into the trace when he's done,
tracking the night upon his hide.

No thanks, no grunts,
even though the hunger
which had stung knots
in his winter gut
lies beneath the red headstone
of his foot-long tongue.

All night we wait full
of ourselves as new graves.

P. B. NEWMAN

The Great Bear

His fur is matted, plenty of ticks
(nothing loves him more, in fact
the only love that equals his)
sucking his blood, the female
swelling like a grape, the pincers
and crawlers disappear, all the while
the male is fucking her, until
she drops, filled with the radiance
of blood and seeds, from the bear vine.

The bear is a tick of a bear.
It takes a bear of a tick to tackle him.
The bear whales the tar
out of anything he likes,
stumps, roots, rivers, tin cans.
He clumps his teeth together
on a number three can of beans.
His teeth leave marks like pistol shots.
He can climb the corner of a chimney
his claws gripping in the cracks
so fiercely that he rises like love
or levitation
in the shelters where the side is open
in the night below the Great Bear.

And the hanging food is there like heaven
only possible to reach by love.
He climbs toward it like ticks toward skin.
The campers whom he loves
are beating on tin pans like bells.
His worshippers in praise.

It is midsummer. Night. In the bunks
they squeeze against the walls
giving him all the room he needs.
They offer up their food. Their kids.
Anything. He is Moloch. He is Baal.
God of the high places and the groves.
God of the solstice and the moon.
God of sacrifice. God of the groin.

VI

O, she will sing the savageness out of a bear!

OTHELLO—William Shakespeare

. . . the master of the house and some of the guests went out of the hut and offered libations before the bear's cage. . . . The housewife and a few old women, who might have nursed many bears, danced tearfully, stretching out their arms to the bear, and addressing it in terms of endearment.

"Killing The Sacred Bear," THE GOLDEN BOUGH

—Sir James George Frazer

The same idea inspired the Siberian hunters' bear-magic down to the eighteenth century. They reverenced the corpse of the dead bear, asking its spirit to go home and tell the other bears how well it was being treated and advise them to come and join it here.

PREHISTORIC AND PRIMITIVE MAN—Andreas Lommel

The Navajo conception of mythology is not very different from the Greek conception of a cycle of plays presenting the myths. . . . the relationship between gods and men. The Navajo expressed this relationship in remembered chants . . . Both onlookers and participants felt that they themselves were involved in the myths, and that their integration with the world of nature and with the spirits was thereby renewed.

NORTH AMERICAN INDIAN MYTHOLOGY—Cottie Burland

'I should say there were little bears, large bears, ordinary bears, and gigantic big bears, all dancing from dark to nearly dawn.'

THE HOBBIT—J.R.R. Tolkien

Even today, a strange music seems to haunt the caves. . . .

"Symbolism in the Visual Arts," MAN AND HIS SYMBOLS

—Aniela Jaffé

Song For The Skull of Black Bear

You came out of pity for my empty mouth
And the wind over my shoulders
As heavy as your paws.
We stood against each other
In the Dance of the Torn Bellies,
But your robe, even without you,
Was heavier than I could carry.
Hung from my neck, your claws
Have shamed my fingers.

Once I was a true hunter
Afraid to speak your name—
Blue Tongue, Old Crooked Foot,
Wearer of the mask Many Bees,
Tree Carver, Honey Snout,
Stands-Like-a-Man, Snow Sleeper
With breath the color of ghosts.
Now I must join you. Now I say
Black Bear, Black Bear.

I have blackened my face
To be your skin, to honor
The thin blood I must give you.
Like your skull in the thick woods
You will hide in the thick of my sleep.
I will dream you and your jaws.
In the Moon of Half-ripeness
You will redden your face to mourn me
When my skull lies by yours.

Hunting Song

When the moon
stays into morning
when the river
calls loudest the dawn
it is our time to hunt
And we hunt
the first bear

Speak Shaman   How do we find
*   the bear*

With the coming of night
build a fire
that you may see my words
With the coming of night
dance by the fire
that you may feel my words

We see Shaman   We see
your words
by the fire
We dance Shaman   We feel
your words
by the fire

      Your bodies grow large
      My words are flesh
      on your limbs
We dance the flesh

      Your skins grow shaggy
      My words are fur
      against the cold
We dance the fur

Your scent grows keen
My words are winds
with their secrets
We dance the scent

You run on fours
Run true on fours
My words are bears
with their secrets
We dance the bear
We dance the bear

Now you know the bear
We dance the bear

You know his ancestors
We dance the bear

You know his trails
We dance the bear

When the moon
stays into morning
you will catch the bear

Etude

Another night of lunacy!
Another full and drunken moon
And I the dwarf and she the bear
To animate the sad cartoon.

It's too bad she's an animal—
A trained observer of my ways
Forced to amuse an unskilled mob
Expectorating whistling praise.

She doesn't even hibernate
But helps me grub along all year—
Living off peanuts tossed to her
—A bleak comedian, I fear.

Just watch her playing. She performs
The lies she memorized from me
So well that she believes and thrives,
In fact, grows fat from phantasy . . .

Another night! My bear, my work,
My huge, well-meaning last big chance
The spotlight of the moon is on
Us once again. Don't fail me: dance!

First Dance: God Who Walks Like
A Bear from *Three Power Dances*

a great Female Bear
    wide as a house   sings
out of Her dark cave
    under Her fringed roots   sings
    up from Her furred clutch   sings
    that hides the mouth of Her hunger sings
out of Her sounding womb hung
    with vines warming the honey   sings
        sweetheart let Me grieve you
            with a new music
        made of old men's bones
            loosen your tongue
            loosen your blood with music
        too stiff to move with Me
            walk you from note to note
        thick at the joints with knobs
            bang our sweet bones together
        sweetheart let Me empty you
            hollow you out with moving
        cric crac cric crac
        I am too old to dance with you
        but I will dance you a pretty dance
        cric crac
        sweetheart let Me skin you
            with rhythms of My touch
        My furred shapeless hands
            so soft you'll never feel
                through brush of my drums
        how the layers slide off you
        to lay you bare to love
        while every stripped muscle cries
        let the old She Bear lie
        down and hold you in Her arms.

115

Song Of The Black Bear

My moccasins are black obsidian,
My leggings are black obsidian,
My shirt is black obsidian.
I am girded with a black arrowsnake.
Black snakes go up from my head.
With zigzag lightning darting from the ends of my feet
    I step,
With zigzag lightning streaming out from my knees
    I step,
With zigzag lightning streaming from the tip of my tongue
    I speak.
Now a disk of pollen rests on the crown of my head.
Gray arrowsnakes and rattlesnakes eat it.
Black obsidian and zigzag lightning streams out
    from me in four ways,
Where they strike the earth, bad things, bad talk
    does not like it.
It causes the missiles to spread out.
Long life, something frightful I am.
Now I am.

There is danger where I move my feet.
I am whirlwind.
There is danger when I move my feet.
I am a gray bear.
When I walk, where I step, lightning flies from me,
Where I walk, one to be feared (I am).
Where I walk, Long Life.
One to be feared I am.
There is danger where I walk.

From A New And Wild Distance

Cold front:
The pregnant Arctic pads,
        growling,
out of the north.
High-pressure mass of polar bear
        tonight!
She'll snuffle through the pines.
        When done
drifting,
        she'll flop
among the sweet azaleas.
        In the crisp morning
still,
        while sleeping in,
she'll nurse our plaid and wooly-padded babies.
        They'll rumple up her covers,
        roll about and play.
Now and again,
        from the shelter of her
        crystal claws and massive haunches,
our winter babies
        will turn toward us and laugh
        in steamy-bright halations.
Her winter babies
        will observe us from
a new and wild distance.

For John And Lucy

aha! spring's a
long way off. the
bears shuffling into
caves. the world
slowing down, the
days gray. one
last fling 'til
sun comes back,
one more time
touching, feeling,
the wedding bells
will ring.
        the
bears find their
way slowly, they
do not choose quickly,
they spend the
year opting for
this berry, this
particular salmon.
ah, but when the
choice is made!
oh, most true of
all the zoo we are,
the bears.
        and
we nose our way
slowly, feeling the
year as few do,
picking the snow or
the spring or the
run of the fish or

the perfection
of the honey straight
out of air. go, let
the dance begin again,
let the cave glow
while the bear and
his lady sing, and
the world turns,
as we do, slowly,
and the spring
begins to build again,
endlessly.   it will
greet you to wake
you soon, and
the world will
bless you, with
all its good things.
amen.

Metamorphic

1

Hallelujah, the thaw!
From the long winter
Sleep I rise.

Where have you been, bear,
Says the breeze. Bear,
Bear, bear, whisper
Green berry bushes.

2

Among bears
I would be known
As the bird, would be taken
For, say, a swallow.
I will lumber aerily
Over timberfall: lichen: fern
As though a bear had grown
On hollow bones.

13:IV:72

april winter
mud /
white &
bone chill
we stop in
tire track ankle
water hollow
to hear first
bear hoots
of spring

Wild Honey

In spring when the honey flows in dandelion
and lilac, apple and violet,
I tack a screen cage like my fist
around a cap I fill with last year's honey,
leave a door in it for the honey hungry,
and carry it up on the mountain
to the woods, and sit in the new
green of maple, watch the hickory swell
and burst through its flowering
cherry bud and wait for a single bee
to find me from a distance I cannot hear,
land loudly on my open lure,
find the cup and fill itself heavy
on its wings and lumber a line toward home.
I watch him disappear, and fix the spot
and go there to wait for another
to read the drunken dance of surfeit,
the shake and beat, the loop and line,
this way, this way, not far, brothers,
fly as I dance. Not long and a second
cuts its engine on my fist and climbs in.
This time I close the door and carry him
a long way on the line, deeper to the heart
of the bee home, release him and watch
his line, and run now, like the honey dance,
leaping and dodging, this way, this way,
deeper and lose it, drop panting
in the old leaves, like the trillium and pulpits,
and wait for the hum of more bees to trap
and carry as far as I can reckon, and run
again following the honey jive, the bump
and lurch, again and again
until shred shirted and scratch sided,
sweat burning my eyes like bright pollens
so I am running by sound alone, learning the dance

at last, I come home to the loudness
of myriads of bees, the hive tree,
terminal and source, politic of comings and goings.
I am the bandit enemy of the state,
if it knew how well I will mark this place
to return in winter while they lie imbedded
in their frozen honeyed sleep. I will come
in snow and ice with bucket, knife, and saw,
climb up and saw out a block,
hack it free and cut out the naked hive,
cut away the amber candy sheets
and leave them in the snow,
honey numb, to freeze and die.

In my dark bear, honey laden sleep, I dream
how the bees will smell me out, lured
to the golden crystals on my beard
and fly back dancing for their brothers
until they all come and cover me bristling
and buzzing like a blanket and eat
the honey from my cloyed lips,
my drowsly drunken flesh, tear
the wings from my eyes, fill me
like a hive, with a spring swarm,
with a new queen.

The Bear's Blessing

In the day of clouds and cold and snow
I will take power from the sun
and dance around you.
I will touch my skin to your skin
and this shall be a blessing to you.

I will give you the cedar tree
the green cedar that never grows old
to have with you against the lightning
and this shall be a blessing to you.

As the fur of my body has touched you
you shall not grow cold
and this shall be a blessing to you.

A SELECTED BIBLIOGRAPHY

Adams, Richard. *Shardik*. New York: Simon & Schuster, 1974.

Bosworth, Anne. "The Man Who Married A Bear," in *Legends of Wilderness Journey*. Utah: American National Enterprises, Inc.

Brooks, Cleanth, and Robert Penn Warren. *Understanding Poetry*. New York: Holt, Rinehart & Winston, 1976.

Bullfinch, Thomas. "Callisto," in *Bullfinch's Mythology*. New York: Macmillan, 1973.

Burland, Cottie. *North American Indian Mythology*. New York: Tudor, 1965.

Carpenter, Rhys. *Folk Tale, Fiction and Saga in the Homeric Epic*. Berkeley: Univ. of California Press, 1968.

Cherr, Pat. *The Bear in Fact and Fiction*. New York: Crown, 1967.

Crane, Stephen. *Sullivan County Tales and Sketches*, ed. R.W. Stallman. Ames, Iowa: Iowa State Univ. Press, 1968.

Crews, Frederick C. *The Pooh Perplex: A Freshman Casebook*. New York: Dutton, 1963.

Crockett, David. *Davy Crockett's Own Story*. New York: Citadel Press, 1955.

"East of the Sun and West of the Moon," in *The Blue Fairy Book*. Ed. Andrew Lang. New York: Dover, 1965.

Engel, Marian. *Bear*. New York: Atheneum, 1976.

Frazer, Sir James G. "Killing the Sacred Bear," in *The Golden Bough*. New York: Macmillian, 1951.

Hallowell, Alfred I. *Bear Ceremonialism in the Northern Hemisphere*. Philadelphia: Univ. of Pennsylvania Press, 1926.

Harding, Esther M. *The 'I' and the 'Not-I'*. Princeton: Princeton Univ. Press, 1965.

Harrison, Jane, and Hope Mirrlees, trans. *The Book of the Bear*. London: Nonesuch Press, 1926.

Hendricks, W.C. "Bear Hunt in Reverse," in *The Bear Went Over the Mountain: Tall Tales of American Animals*, ed. Robert B. Downs. New York: Macmillan, 1964.

Hoagland, Edward. *Red Wolves and Black Bears*. New York: Random House, 1976.

Jones, Gwyn. *Kings Beasts and Heroes.* London: Oxford Univ. Press, 1972.

Lewis, C. S. *Prince Caspian: The Return to Narnia.* New York: Macmillan, 1975.

Lincoln, Abraham. *The Collected Poetry of Abraham Lincoln.* Springfield, Ill.: Lincoln & Herndon Building and Press, 1971.

Lommel, Andreas. *Prehistoric and Primitive Man.* New York: Harry N. Abrams, 1967.

Marshack, Alexander. *The Roots of Civilization.* New York: McGraw-Hill, 1972.

Merriam, C. Hart. *Review of the Grizzly and Big Brown Bears of North America. North American Fauna* No. 41. U.S. Dept. of Agriculture, Bureau of Biological Survey. Washington: Government Printing Office, 1918.

Merwin, W. S. "East of the Sun and West of the Moon," in *The Dancing Bear.* New Haven: Yale Univ. Press, 1954.

Miller, Joaquin. *True Bear Stories.* Portland, Ore.: Binfords and Mort, 1949.

Milne, A. A. *The House at Pooh Corner.* New York: Dutton, 1928. *Winnie-the-Pooh.* New York: Dutton, 1926.

Mooney, James. from *Myths of the Cherokee,* in *Mythology: The Voyage of the Hero,* David Adams Leeming. New York: Lippincott, 1973.

O'Connor, Flannery. *Wise Blood.* New York: Farrar, Straus & Cudahy, 1962.

Olsen, Jack. *Night of the Grizzlies.* New York: Putnam, 1969.

Ovid. *Metamorphoses.* Trans. Rolfe Humphries. Bloomington: Indiana Univ. Press, 1972.

Poirier, Richard. *A World Elsewhere: The Place of Style in American Literature.* New York: Oxford Univ. Press, 1966.

Riley, James Whitcomb. "The Bear Story," in *The Best Loved Poems of James Whitcomb Riley.* New York: Blue Ribbon Books, 1906.

Rubin, Louis D., Jr. *William Elliott Shoots a Bear.* Baton Rouge: Louisiana State Press, 1975.

"Snow White and Rose Red," in *The Blue Fairy Book*. Ed. Andrew Lang. New York: Dover, 1965.

Stem, Thad. *The Animal Fair*. Charlotte, N.C.: Heritage Printers, 1960.

Stevens, James. "The Story of Tuan MacCairill," in *Irish Fairy Tales*. London: Macmillan, 1920.

Taylor, James. *Seeing a Bear*. Pueblo, Colo.: Poetry Bag Press, 1972.

The Three Bears. Illus. Paul Galdone. New York: Seabury, 1972.

Thorpe, Thomas Bangs. "The Big Bear of Arkansas," in *American Literature*, ed. Richard Poirier and William L. Vance. Boston: Little, Brown, 1970.

Tensas, Madison (Henry Clay Lewis). "The Indefatigable Bear-Hunter," in *Southern Stories*, ed. Arlin Turner. New York: Rinehart, 1960.

Tolkien, J. R. R. The Hobbit. New York: Ballantine, 1973.

Utley, Francis Lee, Lynn Z. Bloom and Arthur F. Kinney, ed. *Bear, Man, and God: Seven Approaches to William Faulkners'* THE BEAR. New York: Random House, 1964.

White, T. H. *The Bestiary: A Book of Beasts*. New York: Putnam, 1960.

Bear Crossings was cast into type on the Monotype and printed letterpress by Heritage Printers, Inc., Charlotte, N. C. The typeface is Cochin. The book was bound by The Delmar Company, also of Charlotte. The paper, bearing the watermark of the S. D. Warren Paper Company, has been developed for an effective life of at least 300 years.